MY FIRST YEAR OF BEING A WIDOW
SHARED IN LETTERS TO A FRIEND

From We to Me

by

Maryann Hartzell-Curran

the Peppertree Press
Sarasota, Florida

ISBN: 978-1-61493-160-7

Library of Congress Number: 2013903857

Printed in the U.S.A.

Printed May 2013

For Herschell

Until we meet again

on the Rainbow Bridge.

Table of Contents

Foreword

On August 12, 1998, at nine o'clock in the evening, I became a widow. Eight years after his diagnosis of cancer, my beloved husband, John, died peacefully in the arms of his family. No more pain; no more medicine; no more appointments. The struggle was over, and our life together had stopped. I was now alone. Instead of WE, there was ME.

Now, years later, I am writing letters to one of my most long-standing and dearest friends. Her husband died in 2011 from complications of COPD. After her phone call relating the details of his passing, I decided that I wanted to help her by sharing my stories about living without my husband. This friend, Eddie, is blind, but has a voice-activated e-mail system. This form of communication was decided upon, she accepted the idea, and I began.

Included in this volume are fifty-two letters addressed to my friend. They tell my experiences and feelings during my first year as a widow. I also talk about times during John's illness and before his death. With honesty, I try to discuss my good and bad decisions, but above all, I try to walk with her for the first twelve months.

My memories have important messages seen from my point of view, and share the stages of grief I experienced. My walk was full of bumps but also smooth spots, including humor pointed at myself. I emphasized to Eddie that there is no perfect path of grief. Instead, each of us has to go at our own pace, finding our own way and not comparing ourselves to others. Now, let us begin my transition from *WE to ME*.

Dedication

My journey from *WE* to *ME* was full of self-discovery. When I think about the people God surrounded me with, I am thankful. My family, my friends, my counselors, and my dogs supported me in life without John. I thank them for their encouragement, which gave me courage.

Throughout the letters, you will read individual names. I decided to keep them in my writing, hoping to identify their importance and special contributions. My son, J.T.; my daughter-in-law, Kelly; and my longtime friends Gwen, Joanne, Sara, Candy, Monica, Cathrine, Lyn, Ann, and Diane provided a security system on the rough days, as did my new friends, Mary Jane, Connie, and Nancy, who became part of my future in Florida.

I thank Pastor Jacobs for his many reassuring phone calls. I am thankful for my sister, Susan, and my brother, Russ, who grew up as part of the love story John and I shared. I am also thankful for my in-laws, who shared their son with me for many years. And special thanks go to Linda, John's youngest sister, who experienced the last day of her brother's life.

My dogs, Herschell and Henrietta, played a huge role in my recovery. They were my "family" before I met my second husband, Jack. Little did we know how our lives would change when we met at a bon voyage party on a New Year's Eve cruise. I know that God nudged the two of us together, and Jack's love has been a beautiful blessing in my life.

Finally, I thank John. I think he would be happy that I share our story. I also thank Eddie and Chuck for their example of a great marriage. All three contributed to this record of my grief journey. The transition from WE to ME was made possible because of their strength, my belief in God, and a vision of life, even after death.

Whether you read this book in its entirety at once or chapter by chapter each week, I hope that you can feel happiness along with the pain. Sharing my journey, first with Eddie, and now with you, is a privilege.

Thank you.

WEEK ONE

The Funeral

My dear Eddie,

Thank you for the beautiful funeral service last Friday morning. The readings, flowing music, and radiant flowers created an atmosphere of magnificence. You and your family obviously worked hard to make this special for all of us as we celebrated Chuck's life. I felt his presence and could see him smiling down on the many people who loved him.

This week is going to seem unbelievably long for you. There will be things to do but hopefully also time to rest. If you have to sit, nap, eat, or cry, just do it. Find a special place just for this, perhaps the chair in your bedroom. Use it as we did for the "timeouts" when the kids were little. It will be a safe place, one you will visit often as you feel—yes, feel.

Eddie, I want to walk with you on your journey of grief. I want to write weekly letters via e-mail, sharing stories. I will try to pass on what I learned in my first year without my husband. I'll probably surprise even myself, remembering those experiences moving from WE to ME.

We have been friends for a long time. It is an honor for me to share these letters with you. So let us begin, my friend.

Love,

Mary

Week Two

Halloween

My dear Eddie,

Today is Halloween. I guess you could count this as the first holiday without Chuck. As you know, this year will be a year of firsts. Each first will hold memories, challenging you with poignant reminders of times gone by.

Now let's talk about Halloween. I don't know if you remember, but when J.T. was six, we came to your house to trick-or-treat. I was feeling lonely because John was late coming home from work. He had promised to go with us, but could not, so we left on our own.

A few of the neighbor kids joined us as we marched down the streets. The costumes they wore lent little warmth on that cold, blowy evening. We all arrived at your house, our arms extended with bags still unfilled.

You welcomed us with such joy! I think you were enjoying this activity as much as the kids were. Your porch light was a shiny beacon of warm light as the storm clouds began to drop hail and snow. We left hurriedly, but happy because of your friendly attitude. Later in the evening, as we poured out candy treasures, I silently thanked you.

Now, years later, living in an older community, we probably will have few trick-or-treaters. I think we miss that fun and excitement of our children. We shared those great times as neighbors . . . who became friends.

When you and I talked on Saturday, you mentioned how lonely the house was this week. You also mentioned how quiet the rooms were, but mostly how you missed your husband. Yet you shared good memories of your pajama days, when the two of you would eat bowls of ice cream in bed while watching movies.

Sounds like you had some great together time while he was adjusting to being sick. I do think that accepting sick is a monumental change, especially in a man's life. I think they always want to care for us, but when they get sick, we have to care for them. Those were tough days, yet looking back, I am sure you would not have traded them for anything, except his being healthy again.

By the end of our conversation, you sounded a little lighthearted. I hope you enjoyed the rest of your day with your daughter. You will cling to your children more this first year—and they, to you.

I hope you rest well this week. I am thrilled you are going back to school. I think the time away from home will make your days go a bit faster. My prayer is for that.

Until next week, dear friend,

Week Three

Birthday Party

My dear Eddie,

I remember the surprise party you had for Chuck's sixtieth birthday. It was several months after John died. Your family insisted I come, so I did!

What a successful surprise you had for Chuck. The food, cake, and music were great. The highlight of the evening was when you and Chuck danced to Lady in Red. Dressed in a lovely red dress, you moved like one as the two of you glided around the dance floor. It was a great memory that I am reliving years later.

I am glad we have parties to celebrate our lives. I think you and I would agree that bringing family and friends together renews our love for one another. I think your party paid great tribute to Chuck's life, acknowledging his roles as husband, father, friend, and Christian. Thank you!

We are now in week three; you have accomplished another first, Chuck's birthday. In time, you will celebrate past memories like the one I described, but for now, live in the moment. Take each day as it comes, and please let people help you. You have been there for many, including me, so now it's your turn. Until next week.

Love,

Mary

First Thanksgiving and Christmas

My dear friend,

I hope you had a good weekend. I remembered that your son was coming for a visit. I hope you could lean on his big, strong shoulders for a while. He is a good man, Eddie, and has always been special to our family.

Today, I want to talk about the upcoming holidays. Just want to share a little story.

As you know, John died in August. I got through several firsts: Labor Day, my birthday, and Halloween. Thanksgiving loomed ahead, followed by Christmas. On Thanksgiving, I ate what I could at a small family dinner. For Christmas Day, my daughter-in-law's family invited me. I took my car, drove slowly, and made it through the festive meal. Then, when the beautiful dessert was served, followed by an announcement to go into the living room for gifts, I lost it.

Asking for my coat as her parents begged me to stay, I walked down the hall. Tearfully, I made my way to the front door. My daughter-in-law stated protectively, "I do not think Mom H. should have to do anything she doesn't want to do this Christmas." I was so indebted to her for rescuing me, and the fact that she called me Mom was a wonderful Christmas present.

I drove home, crying, and went to bed early. I got up the next day knowing I had made it through Christmas.

Looking back, I felt blessed to have had so much love, support, and care from my family.

Now, Eddie, let yourself be embraced as you prepare for the holidays. We know you will make it through with God's comforting shoulders to lean on.

Loving you,

Mary

WEEK FIVE

Thanksgiving Plans

My dear friend,

You are now entering week five. It's hard to believe for me; perhaps, you too. It seems the world is ready to celebrate the holidays, with television ads promoting the latest things. I guess the word "things" is exactly what they are, and this year, they are not important.

I will be interested in hearing about your plans for Thanksgiving. Perhaps the kids will come. Perhaps you will go to neighbors. Perhaps you will dine at a restaurant. I hope that your appetite has held steady, but it probably has not. Mine did not, and I did not diet, for the first time in my life. The food just tasted different.

When I think of my blessings, I think of the friendship you and I share. We have traveled many roads in all the years of knowing each other. My hope for you is as few bumps in this new road as possible. I wish for you memories of your blessings with Chuck. They are priceless right now and will be forever.

Take care, dear Eddie. I thank God for you.

Mary

Making a Plan

Dearest Eddie,

As I have written in earlier letters, having a plan for special days really helped me. A recommendation from both my counselors was to prepare for special anniversary dates. Having a plan for that day, even if not carried out, gave me a direction. Another word might be "control."

Sometimes my plan involved other people; sometimes, just myself; oftentimes, my dog. Sharing with him was easier because he understood me differently. I didn't have to banter back and forth. I could just be. That was a gift to me from my Herschell.

In my counseling sessions, we made a plan. Spending time talking about special days when John was alive made me happy. That happiness remained in my mind when the actual anniversary date dawned, and along with my daily plan, that got me through a special day.

There were days when the plan seemed impossible. Sometimes my energy level was low or I was not feeling well physically. Actually, when I look back, I was very healthy, free from a lot of maladies that year. Do not ask me why; perhaps my love for John was kind of a medicine that kept me safe. Anyway, I think I was fortunate with that blessing.

What is that old saying? "Life happens while you are making other plans!" Interesting, isn't it? As my letters continue, you

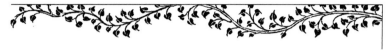

will understand how I utilized planning on many days. That's great advice given to me by caring counselors.

Loving you,

Mary

Quiet House

My dear Eddie,

By now your kids and grandkids have left; the house is quiet, and you start week seven. I am thinking about you, dear friend, and I am proud of you. Hearing your voice when I called on Wednesday gave me a warm feeling. I think we could always talk. That is a great thing!

I know over these last few days, you have had many different thoughts and emotions. I was always surprised when I thought I had a real grip on my grief, then suddenly tumbled down a hill of despair. However, like Jack and Jill, I recovered, picking myself up, feeling calmer after crying. I truly believe crying washes you clean. Perhaps that is why God created tears.

I think having your children near empowers you. Feelings are shared through telling stories and having meals together. The house provides familiarity for all, built with walls of memories. Each time you gather as time goes by, new memories will be made, and the pain will lessen. As you continue your walk, take care of yourself. Rest, good food, and a glass of wine help in your healing. All of these are necessary ingredients, the wine sometimes like a bandage on your pain. I believe everything works together as you walk on this new road.

So, dear Eddie, have a good week, knowing you are loved.

Mary

Christmas Shopping

My dear Eddie,

I hope you survived our huge rainstorm. It poured all night, but this morning the sun appeared over the trees to the east. Good sign!

I thought about you when I was Christmas shopping. I remember the first Christmas without John. Several memories are very clear, and I thought you would like to hear one of them.

I went to Carson Pirie Scott to buy aftershave for my son and my brother-in-law. The department was on the lower level next to the men's apparel. Taking the escalator allowed me to see the beautiful decorations in the store. A grand piano, complete with a wonderful pianist, was set up on the mall level.

As I listened to the music, I felt myself getting sad. By the time I got to the aftershave counter, I was barely walking. The clerk asked me what fragrance I was looking for and reached down under the cabinet. Instead of bringing up the one I had requested, he produced the fragrance John had worn. Well, I burst into tears! I had no tissues, and I was fumbling in my purse, trying to recover my composure. The kind clerk offered his handkerchief, peering at me with soft eyes. After that, I told him my story. When I had finished sharing, tears streaked his cheeks.

A few minutes later, the song "Silent Night" played over the loudspeaker. Do you remember when we sang it at John's funeral? By this time, I had settled down. Deciding to accept the timing of this beloved piece as a sign from John gave me comfort. The words "all is calm" produced tranquility. The kind clerk finished the transactions as I gave him back his handkerchief. While carrying my packages out of the store, I felt grateful for his compassion.

Remembering the Gift of the Christ Child continues to give me joy. After all, if He had not been born, our lives, especially in sorrow, would be almost impossible. Christmas makes all things possible, giving us, and the world, Hope.

Loving you, my dear friend,

WEEK NINE

The Empty Chair

My dearest friend,

I thought this was a good time to insert a story not related to the holidays. This took place on my first trip without John. I know you will relate to its message.

I did go on a cruise with our dear friends in October 1999. We had traveled frequently together, so I felt comfortable with them, and they, with me. The trip was one John had wanted to take; the Panama Canal was the destination.

The first evening, we met our tablemates. When we started to be seated, Lyn and Larry sat next to me on my right, and an empty chair was on my left. Without hesitation, Larry acknowledged this and promptly pulled the chair out, asking the dining room manager to remove it from the table. The whole table was hushed as we made our introductions.

I still revel in his kindness and perception of my emotions. The empty space was filled in as we all moved our chairs into a closer circle. During the evenings we spent together, the table remained set for seven, not eight. Each night, I became more comfortable and glad I had decided to travel again.

The most difficult evening was the formal night. All the men were handsome in their dark suits or tuxedos. The aftershave scents were pungent, and the air lent a feeling of excitement. I think the fantasy on a cruise is like dressing up when we were little children. For a few hours, we can

be Cinderella and her prince. John and I had always loved those special evenings.

However, we were no longer we. Instead, it was me, trying to find my identity in a couple's world. Of course, as the years went by, this became easier, but the first trip was tough. Overhearing an angry conversation between a man and his wife made me exit quickly one evening. The choice I made was to return to my room, skipping dinner. It was the right one because I would have given anything to have my marriage back.

A few hours after I had gone to my cabin, Lyn came knocking on my door. I was out on my balcony when she came. I left the balcony doors open, curtains flying, and with tears streaking my face, I answered the door. She took one look at me and exclaimed, "Oh, no, we will see you at break-fast tomorrow morning!" When I looked at the room, seeing the open door, I could understand her panic and concern. Of course, I did not intend to hurt myself!

On the final day, as we waited at the airport, I had for-gotten a bag in the ladies room. Realizing my passport was in its contents, I panicked. After frantically running back, checking security, and leaving a message, suddenly we were called to the plane. I informed Lyn and Larry about what I had done. We had to board, so we did.

As I sat in my seat, terrified about entering my country without a passport, the plane started up its engines. Just before the door closed, a hustling flight attendant came rushing down the aisle. "Is there a Mary Ann Hartzell aboard?" she yelled.

"Yes, I'm here!" I exclaimed.

As her eyes locked into mine, she proudly handed me the lost bag with my precious passport. "Take care," she said.

My relief and thanks are still hard to describe as I mumbled, "Thank you."

Then I stood up and looked to the ceiling. "Thank you, John," I called out.

At that moment, the people around me clapped, Larry ordered a double scotch, and I could hear John saying, "What did I always caution you about? Take care of your things." Those words were music to my ears as I cried in relief.

The poor man next to me just sat there. He probably wished there was another seat, but there was not. Instead, after a few drinks, he told his story. Divorced, sad, and alone, he confided in me. I listened but clung to my passport—also the memory of my marriage. Peace settled in around me, and I slept soundly.

Eddie, this was my first trip without John. I know you will relate to it as you begin to travel alone.

Love you, dear friend,

Mary

Traveling Alone

My dear friend,

It's already week ten for you! Hard to believe, isn't it? I hope you are back home and settled at your house. I know walking through the front door after being gone brings mixed feelings. Many memories flood your mind, but overall, it's a kind of welcome. My friend Connie once said, "Coming home is like a friend putting [his or her] arms about you and holding you close." A beautiful thought!

I remember traveling without John and how different things were for a long time. His presence now missing, I never really understood all that my husband did while we were en route to a destination.

About a year after I bought my little house in Florida, I was flying home in the late afternoon. We had just taken off for Chicago from Atlanta, and I was sitting in an aisle seat. I thought I was okay, and then all of a sudden, I started to cry. The tears were coming so fast, I think from my toes. By this time in my grief journey, crying like this could happen anytime. I learned just to let the tears fall as I looked for a tissue in my purse.

I heard a quiet voice several seats back. Turning my head, I met the eyes of a young, college-aged boy. He said, "Ma'am, are you all right?"

Well, I was touched and also appreciative while reassuring

him I was okay. I think of that kindness often, feeling he was a gift at a tough time.

Yesterday, on our way to church, we stopped at a traffic light. While waiting for the red to turn green, I observed a man sobbing into his handkerchief. His car was next to ours, and the passenger side was empty. My storytelling frame of mind decided he too had suffered a personal loss. I wish I'd been able to comfort him as I had been comforted.

Here's to the gift of people who appear at times in our grief, helping immeasurably, only to disappear. I know God sends them as His messengers, and for that, I am truly grateful.

Love you, dearest friend,

Mary

New Year's Eve

My dear Eddie,

Tonight is the eve of the new year, 2012. I thought I would wish you a new year greeting. I neglected to use the word "happy." I know you will be happy again, but this will take time. I thought I would share another story.

The second New Year's Eve after John died, I had a little party at the house. This was a big event because it was the first holiday gathering I planned on my own. The house looked festive with decorations and a Christmas tree. Everyone seemed to have a good time, so this was another first for me.

The next morning, New Year's Day, January 1, 2000, arrived quietly. Though I was tired, I drove to the cemetery. During the night, a huge snowstorm had blanketed the earth. Finding the headstone was a challenge, and it was visible only because of colorful Christmas decorations from the previous week.

I took a party hat, some ringers, and confetti to add to the existing holiday theme. After parking my car, I trudged through the thick, wet carpet of white. Afterward, I walked in my own footsteps back to my warm car. Misty-eyed, I glanced back as I drove away, calling out a "Happy new year" to the sleeping cemetery.

Several days later, I returned in the early evening. The air was calm, and an early moon was just appearing to shed cold light on frozen ground. My kids had called, saying

they too had visited on New Year's Day. Stopping my car, I was left wondering. All I saw was one set of footprints. Where were theirs?

Later I called my son. Confused, I asked him, and he exclaimed, "Mom, we walked to Dad's grave in your foot-prints. We just followed your path to and from our car." I was relieved and touched by his explanation.

I thought about this. How comforting, Eddie, to walk in someone's prints, to know that someone went first, making a path for us, like Chuck for you and your family. My dear friend, I pray that all your footsteps lead you to the security of God's love along with the memory of your devoted husband.

Here's to you, my dear friend. A toast to the new year!

Mary

WEEK TWELVE

Post-Christmas

Good morning, dear Eddie,

I plan to call you today. I want to hear how your visit to Chicago went, plus all your news. I know with this cold weather, you have been inside more than usual. We have too, but always seem to keep busy. Anyway, I hope you are well.

Believe it or not, we are in week twelve! That is three months, including big holidays, such as Christmas and New Year's. I remember counting the days after John died. By the time I got to one hundred, it was too hard to keep them straight. I thought with you, counting weeks would be easier.

I do not know how your conversations went with old friends back home. I remember conversations with well-intentioned people. I received comments like, "But didn't you expect this?" "I can't believe you booked that cruise knowing John was sick" was another. To each question or comment, I usually responded by shrugging my shoulders and uttering, "But we never gave up or lost hope!"

Remember what would become Chuck's last day? As you watched the sunrise over the ocean, I thought what he said to you was perfect. "What better place to be than seeing the sunrise over the ocean next to a golf course?" Now looking back, it could have been preparation for his going to heaven later that day. What beautiful words!

I think that hope was a big part of your life, along with the courage you both displayed though he was sick. I know these two components continue in you. They are a part of you even though you no longer are a couple. I believe that your strength will be an asset in your healing. You will heal. This I promise you!

Dear friend, I hope you have a good day, capped off by a radiant sunset, a cold glass of wine, and knowing how far you have come. I am proud of you, Eddie.

Loving you always,

Looking For Him in Familiar Places

My dearest friend,

Today, I wanted to talk about the pain of looking in familiar places for your husband. It took me a long time to sit in our family room across from John's recliner. I made excuses to avoid being in there, choosing the sunroom or living room instead. Then, around the one-year anniversary of his death, I bought new furniture, making things different with the redecoration.

On a cold January evening six months after John had died, my son stopped by on his way home from work. We had set up this ritual on Thursdays in case there was something around the house that needed fixing. I had been expecting him and had my list of little chores, but did not hear the garage door go up by the back door. I was a bit startled as I walked toward him because in that instant, with his back to me and dressed in his father's black leather jacket, I thought John had come home.

Tears stinging my eyes and the unreality of such a thing happening stopped me in my steps. As my son turned toward me, I know he saw surprise, maybe fear, on my face. We embraced as he held me up in physical support. It was so good to see him!

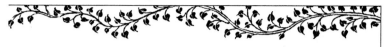

To this day, I will not pass a Doritos display or corn curl container without thinking about the past. Songs from the fifties, a boat harbor bobbing with boats, or a Christmas card from old friends brings memories like an ocean wave. These little things, including his favorite foods, bring back a flood of feelings.

Yet I believe there will always be constants from our life together. Part of grief recovery, I think, is accepting that fact. You will not, nor can you, have the same thing again. Making this part of your thought processes will allow you to open your heart in the future.

My dearest friend, though these memories can be painful, they also give a security. They are special bonds forever that hold a couple together even though they have physically parted. Someday, they will bring smiles; also, tears of joy. To say, "Yes, I shared that with my husband" is a keepsake in your heart forever.

Have a good week, Eddie.

Love,

Mary

Signs

My dear friend,

I remember my first sign from John. The morning of his funeral, three days after he died in our bedroom, I stepped into the shower. The warm water engulfed me, making lots of noise, but also feeling soothing on my skin. My hair had not been washed for days, and my facial skin was dry from all the tears.

As I was rinsing, I felt a breeze behind me. A shiver came over me, making me cold. Increasing the temperature of the water for the remaining time didn't help. When I stepped out, I almost expected John to be standing there. The breeze had been gentle on my skin, but was gone. After grabbing my towel, I wrapped into its comforting softness, but had to sit down.

Yes, I am sure it was a sign. First, John loved to see me dripping wet, stepping out of the shower. Secondly, I just felt his presence; his spirit was there with me. I could have doubted, but chose not to as I continued to get ready for a very busy day.

When we arrived at the church, there was a beige SUV identical to the one John had driven. My son, daughter-in-law, and I looked at one another. We knew it was not possible, and later finding out the owners were members of our church rather astounded us.

Before the service, our pastor gave a prayer just for our gathered family. After we circled the coffin, we stood holding hands. With my hand resting on John's casket, I felt close to him, with the warmth of his fingers entwined in mine. This experience kept me going throughout those poignant next few hours as we said good-bye to this beloved man.

As the years have gone by, I have received other signs. The one in this story remains fresh in my memory, perhaps because it was the first. I have continued to be thankful for the presence of signs, accepting them as gifts.

Enjoy your signs, dear friend. Know that God has sent them to you because He loves you, and so did Chuck.

Always,

WEEK FIFTEEN

Giving Away His Clothes

My dear Eddie,

Here we are in week fifteen. Wow! It's been almost four months, and it's the end of January. Like all the other years, 2012 will go fast, but this year, as you know, *is* different.

Perhaps you have already started to sort clothing, jewelry, and Chuck's favorite things. In today's letter, I want to share stories about my experience doing just that.

Four months after John died, my friend Ethel agreed to help me with the sorting. She was the perfect partner because we were not related and her connection to these things was not personal, except that she loved us. She came on Tuesdays for four weeks. We began to tidy things up and put items into labeled boxes. I had already given my son his father's watch, the family ring, and precious photos.

We started with the clothes closets. John had many baseball hats, so these filled four boxes. I gave a few to close friends, along with several of his colorful ties. Various patterned "happy" ties were hanging on the tie rack. We carefully sorted these and boxed what I did not give to friends and relatives. As the weeks continued, the boxes increased in numbers and crowded the back bedroom. We marked each box. Ethel, her husband, a minister, called a neighboring thrift shop. This shop helped clothe new pastors graduating from the local seminary.

This all took a lot out of me. When finally through, we both felt relief and a sense of accomplishment, and called for a pickup. This was essential to me because I did not want to transport these things myself. They promised to send a van the next day.

Weeks later, I received a beautiful thank-you card from a young man. He had been to the store, picking out one of John's ties, a pair of slacks, and a blue oxford shirt from the items we had donated. Having heard the story about our family from the shopkeeper, he said he felt special wearing clothes from an obviously happy man. Of course, that man was John, and I could see him smiling as I read the kind words.

My advice is twofold on this important endeavor. First, have someone help you who is trusted and can make organized decisions. Second, have a pickup done at your home rather than transporting the clothes yourself. I think these two suggestions remove some of the obvious personal pain associated with such a task.

I wish you well as you sort Chuck's clothes. Take time to rest during the process, and do not hurry.

Loving you,

Mary

Lightning Days

Dearest Eddie,

I remember the day, late in the afternoon, after the van had picked up John's clothes. I was sitting in our living room, drinking a cup of coffee. Suddenly, there was a huge rainstorm riveting the house with wind and large hail. It beat against the walls for an hour. Halfway through the storm, a lightning bolt hit the apple tree across the street, literally shattering the tree's body; shredded leaves exploded on the surrounding lawn.

Shaken, but able to finish drinking my coffee, I looked above the damaged tree to see a radiant, glorious rainbow. With tears rolling down my cheeks, I surveyed this beauty. I think rainbows always bring peace to those who witness their majestic colors.

Looking back on this, I believe all of this was a message from God. Like with the story of the burning bush, lightning brought about important change. The actual tree, leaving only a small stump, was gone and now replaced by a rainbow. A year after this happened, the neighbors who lived on that plot of land observed new green leaves. Last year, while visiting our old neighborhood, we passed by and saw a huge apple tree loaded with fruit in the same spot. I know it came back from the day of lightning.

Therefore, Eddie, I guess a good descriptive term for

our tough days is "lightning days." Throughout this grief journey, there will be many days with the promise of many rainbows bringing joy. That joy I wish for you, my dearest friend.

Until next week. Love,

Letting Go

My dear Eddie,

I wanted to offer a final word about the distribution of John's clothes and all the boxes. The Sunday before the pickup, the kids stopped over for lunch. Being proud the day before of all my accomplishments, I awoke angry that morning, near tears, and really disturbed—perhaps even though rationally I knew letting go of his things was the right thing, I was confused.

My wise son must have seen this on my face because he asked me to show him the boxes upstairs. Just he and I climbed up those thirteen steps together.

The room was packed so full that there was only room for us to stand against the wall. We stood quietly. Then I started fidgeting, attempting to pace in the small space and feeling agitated. My child said in hushed tones, "Mom, I think you are really angry today."

Well, like a rocket ready to leave the launchpad, I set off into a rampage of crying, cursing, and calling out to John. "How unfair of you to die!" I screamed. Now when I write these words, I can still feel the release of my feelings. J.T. just stood calmly, watching me pick up shoes, hats, and carefully folded T-shirts. By the time I was through, the room looked like a tornado had passed. Sighing, I sat down on the floor.

Yes, this was really happening. Yes, John had died. Yes, I was letting his clothes go. I look back on those moments, realizing I had entered a new phase of my life, and it was real!

My loving children helped me refold the clothing, place hats back in the boxes, and tape the open lids shut. Then, as a family, we walked out the door, closing this chapter in our family life.

I think it is important that I tell you about this lightning day. Looking back, God has blessed me with many rainbows in my life, both with John and after John. I think the beautiful colors in the rainbow remind me of the fragility of life. One minute, the rainbow is spread across the sky, and the next, it is gone, leaving only a memory.

Loving you, Eddie,

Mary

WEEK EIGHTEEN

Happy Birthday To Me

My dear Eddie,

Happy birthday, my dear friend. Talking to you on Saturday was such fun, and I am sure all who love you, including me, will make your day very special. This is week eighteen, and I want to share my birthday story with you.

John had been gone for almost three months when my October birthday arrived. I was on the Panama Canal cruise that I mentioned in an earlier letter. Spending time touring Grenada and even buying a Lladro look-alike from an apprentice were experiences on this first trip without my husband.

The morning of my birthday, I awoke feeling okay. However, after I got up, I began to feel sad, ready to cry, and very lonely. Suddenly, my nice balcony room felt quiet; I missed my family immensely, and I convinced myself that being on this trip was a mistake. A few tough hours prevailed.

I looked at the phone on my dresser, and the quoted price of $9.95 per minute, and then picked up the receiver and dialed J.T. at his office. The phone rang three times, and was answered by a quiet, elderly voice. I asked for my son. The person who had picked up the call was the owner of the company. As if he knew my feelings, he assured me to hold and he would find him. I waited, waited, and suddenly heard, "Happy birthday, Mom."

Then the tears came. I muttered how sad I was, only stopping to share a peaceful moment as I inhaled. With that, J.T. spoke such important words. He said, "Mom, do you know how proud we are of you? How well you are doing, and that we love you?" I will never forget how thankful I still am to my child.

After nine minutes and a quiet good-bye, we both hung up. Suddenly, I was glad for my birthday. I was ready for my coffee and toast on my balcony. I knew in my heart that John had sent me his birthday gift. My son's wishes, the lovely sunny day, and my birthday memories of the past contributed to a beautiful day.

So Eddie, happy birthday! You, like me, will make a great party, enjoying the moment. Blow out the candles, and know this is yet another first. I believe that today you will receive a special gift from Chuck. As you celebrate with family and friends, look around and see his smiling face in the people who love you.

Enjoy!

Love you,

Mary

WEEK NINETEEN

Valentine's Day

My dear Eddie,

By the time February arrived in 1999, five months had passed without John. The week of Valentine's Day, I had dinner with friends, and decorated John's stone with festive hearts, even balloons! I sent and received valentines. I thought I was ready to face this romantic holiday alone.

It turned out that I wasn't. The day began sad and with the passing hours became sadder. There was no heart-shaped valentine on my pillow or vase of red roses, and there were no plans to go out for dinner. The year before, we had gone to see the movie Titanic, followed by wonderful French food. Not this year! I remember standing in my closet of pretty dresses, crying, sure that my social life had ended.

At about noon, I dressed and drove to the cemetery. The grave looked beautiful on what turned out to be a rainy day. Many cars lined the cemetery driveways. I had gotten to know several families with my frequent visits, so I greeted Mr. Miller as he visited Mrs. Miller. Edith, a young mother whose daughter had died of leukemia that year, waved as she placed a bottle of bubbles next to the grave. We all spent moments in quiet thought, then left separately to go back to our new lives.

Almost spent from the flow of tears, I decided to go to a movie. I picked Saving Private Ryan, perfect for the way my day was progressing! The theater was filled with many World War II veterans, some sitting alone, and others sitting together in small

groups. I had heard that the movie was a great tribute to those who served, but I was not prepared for the graphic representation of death and destruction.

The story, though violent, shared personal love stories. One poignant one was told by Tom Hanks, who played a first lieutenant. When his platoon asked him about his marriage, he said, "I believe there are some things that should remain private and never repeated by a husband or his wife." So his men sat back quietly, lost in their own love story memories. That is when my next wave of tears flowed.

For the remainder of the movie, I sobbed with all of the other people. No one knew my story, and I did not know theirs, yet we shared tears together. I actually liked this setting, where the tears did not have to be dried, but dried on their own.

When I left the theater, I walked out in silence, as did the rest of the audience. This was the kind of movie that left you speechless, with messages very meaningful and personal. Obviously, this was true, as I relate lines from a film I saw over thirteen years ago. I walked out into the cold darkness, feeling calmer as I realized I had made it through my first Valentine's Day . . . without my valentine.

Now, I wish for you great Valentine's Day memories warmed by the love you shared with Chuck. We were blessed to have our husbands' hearts all those years and to be with our husbands when those hearts stopped beating.

Talk to you soon, dear friend,

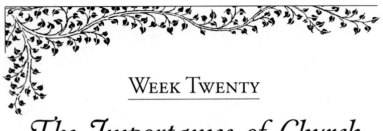

The Importamce of Church

Hi, dear friend,

I hope you had a good week and have plans for the upcoming weekend. Sundays were always so long for me if I was not involved in activities. I thought I would write about Sundays in this letter.

We always went to church on Sunday. Usually, the early service at 8:15 was our family choice but almost punishment after a fun, wine-filled Saturday evening. It was also painful when we had to awaken J.T. Then, after years of this early service, opportunities to worship at a later hour were available. We always sat in the back row near a wall column. I do not know why, but this became our family space.

After John died, I continued to sit there. Sometimes J.T. and Kelly would join me, but most of the time, I went alone. Frequently, I would go to the cemetery to wish John "Happy Sunday" and then drive to church. The cold, rainy, or snowy mornings were the worst ones but were far outnumbered by sunny, beautiful days.

I remember the day that I changed my place at church. Instead of the back row near the column, I sat in the front part of the sanctuary. I was amazed at the different perspective I had sitting there. Feeling foreign, it also felt freeing! After all, this was one of the different ways I now looked at life as I continued to go on from WE to ME.

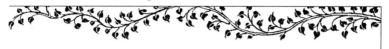

On another day, I called and asked the church secretary to put my name on the mailbox in the narthex. I remember being a greeter before services by myself and then driving home alone. Keeping active was good, but there was no one with whom to share the joy of a great sermon or how beautiful the altar flowers looked that morning. This does sound very sad, but through all of these moments, I knew God was right there, holding my hand. His love gave me courage.

I will always be thankful for my Christian marriage, for our many church friends, for the youth group that John founded, and for the preschool that brought me joy. The Sundays always turned into Mondays that motivated me through another week.

Someone once asked John why we went to church. Interesting question! He pondered for just a moment, answering, "Mary and I need church." I think the fact that there was little hesitation became the true answer.

Have a good week, dear one.

Love,

Mary

WEEK TWENTY-ONE

Ash Wednesday

My dear Eddie,

Well, today is the day after Ash Wednesday. We went to 8:30 Mass yesterday and received our ashes, followed by an emotional homily. Both experiences left me opened up to God's presence in my life. I felt honored to be wearing the ashes, wishing I had been out in public after the service. However, one of our Bible study partners was, and she shared her story.

After Mass, she went to her local bank to make a deposit. As she walked to the teller station, the young man behind the counter looked curiously at her forehead. At first, she said she wondered what he was looking at; then she remembered and smiled. He began to ask her all kinds of questions, including the significance of the ashes, where they came from, etc.

She said the answers seemed to spew out of her mouth with no hesitation. During this time, others in the bank gathered around, seemingly thirsty for the knowledge she was sharing. The smiles on the faces of the crowd made a huge impression on her as she told of the new promises from Jesus. Here was a real witnessing story.

I think, Eddie, that the walk you are walking is also a witness. The love you have for your husband and family, provoked by the love of God, is a testimony in itself. The experiences you shared in your marriage and have now on your

own are direct reflections of your faith and knowing there is a heaven where we will rest eternally.

I believe that when this first year is over, it will be over with all of the firsts completed. I promise you peace in your second year, a peace we have already seen in you these last few months. You will continue to teach many around you how to do this—and do it well.

Love to you, my dear friend, in yet another first. Lent, along with all its ponderings, is upon us, provided by God's grace.

Talk to you soon.

Love,

Mary

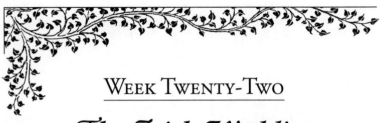

The Irish Wedding

Dear friend,

We have just returned from our week in Ireland. I told Jack that of all our many adventures traveling, this will remain one of my favorites.

The real reason for this trip was an invitation to a wedding in Clifden, Ireland. A grade school—yes, grade school—friend of Jack's invited us to his youngest daughter's celebration. We really did not intend to go, but as the date got closer, we accepted. I am so glad we did!

'Twas a gala event. Held in a tiny stone Catholic church that seated only sixty people, the service was conducted by a young priest, Father Patrick. Fresh lilies, daisies, and rosebuds dressed the windowsills, doorways, and pews. People crowded in, wearing their finest apparel, including women wearing fascinators.

In case you are wondering, a fascinator is a tiny wispy hair adornment with an attaching clip. Feathers, a peacock plume, lace, ribbon, and gauze were materials used in making these little creations. In fact, some of the women made their own original designs. Mine was a pink silk rosette nestled in a bed of soft black feathers. Not homemade, mine came from shopping on Amazon!

After the ceremony, we stood outside, waiting to greet the new couple. A fine, misty rain started to fall from the gray

sky, but this did not dampen the high spirits of our group. I think their happiness was contagious to us all.

Moving on to the reception, we were treated to Prosecco, delicious appetizers, and Irish music, played by local musicians. Fitted into a corner of the colorful, blue-tiled room, lively sounds of violins, even an oboe, filled the air. All of this lent to a party spirit, as I observed several ladies, widows, tapping their feet in time to the traditional songs. All of them were dressed beautifully, and they were waiting to be asked to dance.

Watching, my heartstrings were pulled because I remembered the same feelings when I attended my first wedding without John. When I looked around the room, only a few single men were present.

Almost as if they had heard my thoughts, two by two, the ladies formed couples approaching the dance floor. The music intensified, producing a faster beat, and suddenly the women began an Irish step dance! This was fun to watch, and I understood the happiness this activity promoted, painting new smiles on the dancers' faces. People were having fun!

Afternoon became evening, and the party continued with an elegant dinner served, capped off by decadent desserts. The champagne flowed, more Guinness pints were consumed, and the tables of guests became one in celebration.

When we left, our stomachs were full; our voices hoarse from laughter; and our feet, sore from dancing. I think the young couple started their new life together rooted on by our love and our best wishes. What a great evening!

As I watched, I remembered our children's weddings. John and I attended both your daughters' weddings, and you and

Chuck came to our son's. These were great fun for our families years ago.

My dear Eddie, I thought you would enjoy the Irish wedding story. We are glad we went!

Love you,

Mary

The Puppy and Happy Endings

Dear Eddie,

It's week twenty-three; it's been almost six months. I hope you are keeping busy. A few more weeks, and it will be Easter. I look forward to sharing my first Easter story with you soon.

Today, I thought I would write about happy endings. I know this seems almost inappropriate in its connotation, but it is not. You will understand at the end!

A few days before John died, several of our neighbors and friends had dropped by for the evening. By now, John no longer could walk but was nestled comfortably in our bed. Someone had brought a light supper, so I spread a tablecloth over the sheets, and the bed was our table. I said later that I had never entertained so much in our bedroom!

Around nine o'clock, J.T. and Kelly bounded into the room. Smiles painting their faces, their cheeks pink with excitement, they ran to our bed. J.T. quieted the roomful of people by saying, "We have an announcement to make." Silence ensued! John rolled his eyes, and I held my breath.

"We ordered a puppy!" was the news. Probably a million things crowded my mind. That evening, I was strong in living each moment. I dared not look too far ahead, so I needed to be happy at this time. Of course, they could have announced

just about anything, so the puppy news brought a cheer! Love filled our room, and I know that John felt its warm embrace from all those present. Everyone knew our family loved dogs.

The next weeks went by; we got through all the formalities and sadness. I settled into a quiet house without my husband. Just existing each day brought different challenges, which I handled the best I could. Then, around the first of October, J.T. called, inviting me to meet "the puppy."

It was a Friday evening, with beautiful warm weather and an amazing sunset, and I appreciated sharing its glow as a family. When I arrived, my son and the puppy sprinted out the door. "Mom, meet Mackenzie," J.T. exclaimed.

There before me was a fluffy black and brown puppy leaping with happiness. He jumped into my arms, licking my face as he greeted me. This all filled me with joy.

Later, after some great conversation and good pizza, J.T. and I sat on the living room sofa. He and Kelly had borrowed several pieces of our old furniture for their new home, so sitting together felt familiar and comforting.

We each sat at opposite ends, the puppy romped about, and our hands spread across the back of the sofa. For an instant, our fingers touched, causing me to immediately start crying. All of a sudden, overcome with sadness, I blurted out, "I am so sorry it was not a happy ending."

"Mom, it was a happy ending. Do you know all the happy memories we have as a family? More than I can count. It all will be okay, Mom." These are kind words that I remember vividly years later.

Eddie, our children will touch us. They will hold our hands, and they will assure us as we continue this walk. I

always felt that having a child secured lives forever, even though things could change. The sharing of a child, another human being, is one of life's and death's gifts.

Through this year and the years to follow, they will share memories with you and with each other. Enjoy the stories, and cherish each one, my dear friend.

Loving you,

Mary

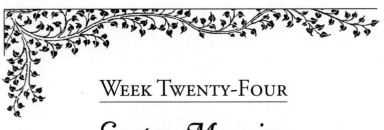

Week Twenty-Four

Easter Morning

My dear Eddie,

I promised you my Easter story. I remember my feelings and a renewal in my belief in the resurrection. Our first Easter without John turned out to be special for many reasons.

The evening before, Holy Saturday, was a beautiful, warm, almost balmy night. In fact, because of its loveliness, I drove to the cemetery. I had already decorated John's grave with a ceramic Easter bunny, a tiny plastic basket, and a pot of red tulips. Everything looked pretty, almost waiting for dawn on Easter morning.

Losing track of time, I got ready to leave. The new, full moon was peeking out of white, puffy clouds. As I drove down the dirt road to go out of the cemetery gates, there in my headlights, lying very still, was a beautiful gray squirrel. Quickly, I got out of my car, leaving the lights on in order to see the little animal.

Indeed, the squirrel was dead. It probably had fallen from the tree branches above. Its presence made me cry. I could tell during that day that tears were welling up inside of me, so I let them roll down my cheeks. I could not just leave him there. After going to the trunk of my car, I removed a roll of paper towels and then gently picked up the body. I wrapped several layers of white, billowy fabric around him so he would not be cold during the night. I left him safely under the tree and drove home.

Easter morning arrived, radiant with a blue sky, singing birds, and sunshine so bright it made me squint! After having my coffee, I dressed for church and left the house earlier than usual. Almost by instinct, I drove back to the cemetery. At first, I felt sad, but as I drove closer, I was sure I could hear John singing in the heavenly Easter choir. This made me smile!

After finally arriving, I walked to the stone, greeted John with a loud "Happy Easter," and glanced over to the trees along the driveway. With memories of the last evening, I stepped lightly. I found the paper toweling, but no sign of the squirrel. Truly, this gave tangible meaning to the real resurrection. Confusion, wonder, and a bit of fear filled my soul.

To this day, I do not know what happened during the night. However, this I do know: Easter makes us aware of the love, protection, and power our faith gives us. Bodies die, but their souls go on. Our Christ has given us that gift of faith. He has given us a place in heaven.

Happy Easter, Eddie.

Love,

Mary

WEEK TWENTY-FIVE

The Monarch

My dear friend,

This afternoon, I looked out the front door and saw a monarch butterfly lying on the sidewalk. Its body was still, with its wings closed. It was perfectly intact as I lifted it from the warm concrete. I recognized it as the busy, happy butterfly that had been flitting around the house for weeks. If indeed it was that one, I will miss watching all of its activity.

The life span of a butterfly is debatable. Several years ago, we visited a butterfly sanctuary housing different kinds of these wonderful creatures. When I asked the guide how long they lived, she said from two weeks to one year. While we stood by the front door, many butterflies were lying on the ground. The guide explained that they fly and fly, then fall and die.

Knowing this information helped me to understand a little bit about this monarch's timeline. I had enjoyed the happiness it exuded, flying from plant to plant. Resting on the house siding, drinking from the birdbath, and surrounding the house daily in swooping flight patterns had entertained us over the weeks. The butterfly just made me happy when I watched, and I will miss it.

I feel honored that it lay on the front sidewalk. It was as if it wanted me to know it was done flying. I remember in Scripture the verse about God's knowing all creatures, even

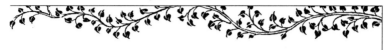

the sparrows that fall from the sky. I look at the butterfly's presence as a gift from God, who lent us its beauty, only to take it back.

I picked up the still body, sensing the final wave of its wings. As I held it in my hand, it seemed to be saying good-bye to me, to life, and to its time on earth. I gently carried it into the house while glancing at the new climbing vine on our fence. There was a green and yellow striped caterpillar, perhaps a new monarch, looking up at me. Maybe we again will enjoy a butterfly after the cocoon forms, protects, and then releases another beautiful life.

This whole experience is emotional for me. I feel privileged to have enjoyed the monarch and hope to enjoy its offspring. Until then, we will just miss it.

Sending my love to you,

Mary

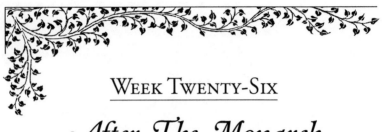

After The Monarch

My dearest Eddie,

Three days after the monarch died, in mid-afternoon, I went out on our front porch to water the flowers. Next to one of the wicker chairs lay another monarch. Its wings were closed, and I gently picked it up, suspecting yet another butterfly was dead. Instead, its wings started to flutter as it struggled to stand up in my hand. It teetered on my thumb, only to walk back into my palm with confidence.

I was overjoyed. At the end of my last story, I had seen a beautiful caterpillar that was potentially a monarch, according to Google. I just did not expect to see a newly formed creature this soon. So I sat down, looking steadily at this sticky, alert, and determined butterfly. After a while, I set it down on some outside pillows.

Its wings were entangled, and because of its struggling, I expected to find it lying on the pavement, done with its life. Thoughts of it being malformed, hit by a car, or even hurt by a hungry bird passed through my mind. With my husband urging me to "just let him be," I returned to my activities.

About an hour passed, with the curiosity in me building, so I finished my gardening and returned to the porch. By now, the monarch had walked to the edge of the pillow, clinging with busy feet to the material. The wind was getting stronger as small gusts swooped down and invited the

monarch's new wings to open. They started to, and I began to feel hopeful again. When we went inside to eat dinner, I left it where it was.

Another hour passed. It was getting dark. Soon the outside lights would go on, and the temperature would drop. The nurturing, mothering instincts in me took over, propelling me out the front door for one more peek. I was really expecting the butterfly to be giving up its desire to fly.

But miracle of miracles, it was gone! Nowhere could I see it. The cushion that had given it comfort was empty. I looked all around but saw nothing. I felt happy and privileged to have witnessed this entire event. The newly formed butterfly had become a full-grown monarch. Now perhaps it was peering at me through palm branches as it rested for the night.

It's Easter morning, and I'm at the window. Yes, you guessed it; a monarch is slowly flying around the porch. It is beautiful and somewhat shiny on the outside of its body, and is coming to perch on the gate railing. I think it is telling me, "Happy Easter," and I am okay and also very happy. I think it could be thanking me for letting it spread its new wings.

So, happy Easter, Mr. Monarch.

Loving you, dear friend,

WEEK TWENTY-SEVEN

The Front Door

My dear Eddie,

As I told you in another letter, I stayed in the family house for two years. Shortly before Christmas of 2000, after having lunch with my son, I blurted out that it was time for me to sell and move to another location. J.T. did not seem a bit surprised. He said that he and Kelly had been waiting for this to happen. Their acceptance, plus my readiness, made the decision right.

I sold our home and bought a townhome in a two-week period. Real estate was at its peak then, so this made life very easy. As I wanted to downsize, a townhome seemed like a good choice. My Realtor showed me a local one for sale not too far from our house. Walking through the beautiful home, I received a sign from John.

There hanging in the hallway was the young owners' marriage announcement. July 22nd blatantly called out to me as their anniversary. Ours was too, except thirty-four years earlier. Later that week, I made an offer, including those numbers. It was never countered, and I signed a contract.

The young owners were eager to leave, and the closing came quickly. The buyers of our family home had to wait a little longer, so I had lots of time to get ready for the move. The night before the moving van was scheduled to come, Herschell and I drove over to the new townhome.

It was a rainy, windy Sunday evening. Lightning flashed across the dark sky, and we went in the front door. Herschell never liked storms, so he followed my every step as we went from room to room. Because there was no furniture, our feet made echoes that created even more noise. Before leaving the upstairs hallway, I sat down to rest on the top step, with Herschell clinging to me.

Our view from that level was beautiful. The high, heavily paned living room windows allowed us to gaze out at the lush landscape surrounding the small lake behind the house. The lighted fountain hummed as it threw water high in the air, and the water made solid splashes as it came back down. That sound and the sound of the continuing storm, with my Herschell shaking by my side, gave me comfort.

In those moments, I accepted all of the change ahead of me. I was peaceful with getting things ready to move, getting items distributed, and giving others away. Those things that would be part of our new home were packed and waiting to create our future. I found myself excited to see how everything would look once delivered.

The next day, after the packed moving van had left for the new house, I stood for the last time in our kitchen. Looking around me, I could hear the "voices" of memories made in this room. All the family dinners, conversations, laughter, and tears were echoing from the walls. I continued through the rest of the house, thinking similar thoughts. Then, looking at my watch, I proceeded down the hallway and out the front door, and locked it for the last time. "Done," "finished," and "ready" were words playing in my head.

I remember being surprised at myself that there were no tears. Instead, I wore a broad smile on my face. I felt hopeful with all of the precious memories from the years we had spent there. Making a new home was my goal for the future. This was important as I changed from WE to ME.

Driving down our street for the last time, I looked in my rearview mirror. Reflected in it was our beloved home and . . . perhaps . . . John waving good-bye. What a great ending to an important time in my life. Now it was time for me to open that new front door!

Eddie, I am thinking of you tonight, sending love and the hope for a key to that new "front door" in your life.

Loving you,

WEEK TWENTY-EIGHT

Anger

My dear friend,

It is very important that I relate my experiences with anger. Looking back, I think anger disguised itself in many ways. Tears, physical and emotional outbursts, fatigue, cynicism, and denial all played a role in my anger. At times, mine cropped up inappropriately, proving to be embarrassing for myself and others.

It is essential that people closest to you during this time identify that such behavior has nothing to do with them. At times, their acceptance must override personal feelings. Grief can keep us out of touch with reality. Remember my story about throwing John's hats? My oversensitivity was hard enough for me, so my target needed to understand for both of us.

In July 1999, eleven months after John died, we attended the wedding of one of J.T.'s high school friends. I went expecting our old friends to hover around me. However, this did not happen.

Walking into the reception alone, I realized there were no assigned seats at the reception dinner. Floundering, near tears, really missing John, I was frozen, not moving. It was a true reality check!

Suddenly, I felt arms around me, with a soothing voice in my ear, saying, "Now, you just come with us."

Glancing back, I recognized the mother of J.T.'s friend Mike, and we walked to a nearby table. Safety spelled itself out as we all sat at the dinner. I felt such relief.

These same loving people had to leave early, so once again I found myself alone at a table for eight. The DJ started playing old songs, rekindling many memories. By eleven o'clock, even though my son had asked me to dance, I left and walked back to the hotel . . . sobbing. I felt abandoned!

The next morning, after breakfast and a restless night, my daughter-in-law and son joined me. We started the drive home, and I insisted on driving. I drove too fast, with the radio too loud, yelling my disappointment about the wedding. I know it was a scary time, even dangerous, as my anger was a catalyst in my grief.

By God's grace, we got home safely, and my family left. I cried the rest of the day and fell asleep fully dressed on our bed. I still called it that, even though now it was my bed. I was a mess!

As the year progressed, similar episodes occurred, but I learned to recognize the signs. Becoming realistic about emotional situations that could set off this anger, I even had the courage to deny some invitations. I felt this decision-making was part of my healing and the transformation of WE to ME.

I think these experiences were necessary to empty my soul of frustrations, disappointment, and the loss of my husband. Slowly, I released the bad stuff, and my journey continued through that rough spot, with fewer outbursts over time. Looking back, I think those "bumps" of anger smoothed the road of recovery.

Dearest friend, until next week.

Lovingly,

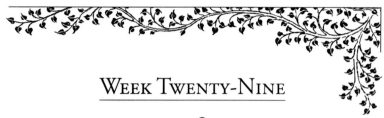

Beloved Health-Care Professionals

My dearest friend,

I hope this finds you well. It's hard to believe that week twenty-nine is already here. I hope that you have found this counting of weeks beneficial. As I shared with you, counting days got exhausting for me.

In reviewing my letters, I have considered the health-care professionals who took great care of us. During the eight years of John's cancer, our favorite doctor was Dr. K. Even when John was in a research program, Dr. K. was our main contact. His encouragement became a beacon of hope, even toward the end of John's life. I know you relate to the love of your doctors because you and I have talked about this over the last few months.

On the day of the funeral, right before we walked out the door, Dr. K. called. He wanted me to know that we had "done everything right." These words calmed doubts I had had, helping in the many hours ahead with my family. His ending words included, "When you are ready to talk, come in and see me." I did six weeks later.

The office staff had scheduled me at the end of a Friday morning. I walked down the familiar hallway, remembering walking with John by my side. The nurse escorted me into a

familiar room. Assuring me the doctor would be in soon, she left me alone. About five minutes passed, and a knock startled me back into reality. He opened the door.

After I hugged him, we sat down opposite each other. For some reason, I felt I had not seen him in years when actually it had been only weeks. He started our conversation by saying, "So, how are you?"

I replied, "Fine." However, I was not! Within seconds, I started to cry, then sob, and though we were across the room from each other, I felt his warmth.

Soon I recovered, and we began to talk. After reviewing the details from the funeral, my family, and things in general, he said something wise. "Maryann, try to get through the emotions of grief the best you can. However, do not be angry too long because John was a happy person who loved you and his family. He gave his best in this battle with cancer, so try to remain optimistic. That was who he was, and he would want the same for his loved ones."

These were important words that have remained strong in my memory all these years. Though the message was meant for me, I wanted to pass this on to you. The words' impact became valuable on many bad, lonely days.

Eddie, I know you had a "Dr. K." in your journey with Chuck. The words of our wonderful doctors are gifts from our husbands, messages that echo in our ears.

Love you, dearest friend,

Gardens Old and New

My dear Eddie,

I hope this finds you well and enjoying our glorious weather. My garden is almost singing since the rain on Monday. If I were to count, I would estimate that there are at least a dozen butterflies surrounding the house. Their presence constantly reminds me of God's love found in simple forms, including the butterfly.

When I am in my garden, I feel happy, even among the weeds! I remember an evening in early spring after John had died. I was sitting out on the back deck, sipping a glass of wine and enjoying the beauty of early nighttime. I could see the pale, white outline of the moon on one side and the golden sunset on the other. Kind of a double treat!

As I sat there, I remembered many springs and the promise of new life. We lived in that house twenty-three years, with changes as the time passed. I looked at the blossoms on the apple tree, a gift long ago for Mother's Day. I gazed at a new garden in the back part of our lot, which had been J.T.'s sandbox for years. I glanced at the hostas our neighbor had lovingly planted in the last year. Also waiting to be enjoyed was my mother-in-law garden. I had filled it with plants from frequent visits to Wisconsin. A rose bush, full and blooming, stood valiantly along the back fence. All was a collection of family memories, now speaking to me this evening.

That garden in Glen Ellyn held memories from our past. My new garden here in Florida is creating memories for the future. Ignited with beauty and tranquility, it promises joy in coming days.

Eddie, I wish for you a happy spring. Perhaps next year at this time, you too will be enjoying a new garden in your new home. I share this hope as you make another transition from WE to ME.

Love you, dear friend.

WEEK THIRTY-ONE

Taking Care of Yourself

My dearest friend,

I hope you are doing well. I think of you often and am glad we are staying in touch. From our talk on Saturday, it sounds like you are eating well, sleeping soundly, and planning activities. I am sure your pool party was a success last week shared with good friends. You go, girl!

In a letter several weeks ago, I mentioned my belief in taking care of you. I think it is fair to say that going through grief is hard work. While experiencing emotions such as anger, sadness, and what some would call "fabricated happiness," it is possible to get through even the toughest days, if you take care of yourself.

As you also know, part of grieving is living alone and the lack of touch. Recognizing that, I planned to have regular facials, pedicures, and manicures. These made me feel pampered but also kept me "in touch" with people. Granted, they were professionals, but they were friends in a different way.

Several times when I went to the spa, I had a tension-filled moment or crying spell. The people at the salon would acknowledge where I was, allowing me to be quiet and accepting me just as I was that day. For this, I will always be profoundly grateful.

When I traveled, I found the courage to state the importance of my privacy. A typical cabin steward on a cruise ship

would react to this with surprise. However, it was my wish, and I appreciated their acceptance. Yet, as I walked past the room stewards, dressed for dinner, at times they would compliment me quietly. I really did cherish this beginning to an evening.

Having my dog Herschell was extremely helpful. He was a responsibility, needing me to feed, walk, and care for him. He cared for me also, but in a different way. When I watched television, he would sit on my lap, sometimes expecting attention. If I did not respond, he was happy to just be with me. He slept right by my side in the huge, king-sized bed, keeping me warm on cold nights. I think if he could have talked, he would have shared many stories!

On my sad days, I still tried to get out of the house for a while. I walked a lot, sometimes with Herschell, sometimes not. Spending time in my garden, enjoying the flowers and feeling the cool leaves in my hands, provided stimulation. All of this soothed me, especially on sunny days, inviting me into their warmth. Herschell could find the tiniest sliver of sunlight and plant himself in it. The two of us spent time enjoying together these simple pleasures of life.

Cooking for me was difficult. For months, shopping was hard, and because of habit, not bringing home John's favorite foods, I became a real TV dinner gourmet! One Saturday at the food store, there was a man standing next to me in the frozen food section. Opening a freezer door, I exclaimed, "Well, this is the way to cook!" Pulling ten separate frozen meals off the shelf and putting them in the cart, I could feel his smiling eyes on my back!

Dearest friend, again, I share some of my "feeling" stories. Looking back, I am thankful that I did feel, even though it

was not easy. You and I are lucky to be sensitive experiencing this grief journey. Someday, like me, you will share your stories and walk with someone. Guiding with your heart is a gift you have, Eddie. I am proud to be your friend.

Love always,

Mary

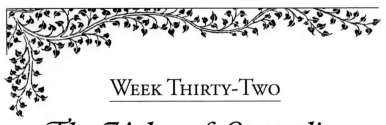

The Value of Counseling

My dearest friend,

Today, I want to talk about the value of counseling. I was blessed with a wonderful grief counselor, who helped me once a week. The cost in dollars was minimal compared with the value of her guidance. I think counseling is an investment in yourself. I know you agree.

Her office was in her home. When I went for my sessions, I walked down the hall to a small bedroom office that served as her therapy room. A candle burned with its fragrance, perhaps eucalyptus, permeating the air. Quiet music from a CD played, and two chairs across from each other accommodated us. I felt at home.

At first, we discussed the physical illness that John had suffered, including all the responsibility associated with the illness and the effects on me. We talked about family, friends, and my volunteer work. I think I was doing more reporting than feeling during this time. Waiting for my deep emotions to come out, she patiently listened, nodding her head as I spoke.

About five months into my therapy, on a cold, rainy morning, she presented the topic of the day. Usually she was not directive in our sessions, but she was that day. My assignment or topic was to describe what it was to be Mrs. John Hartzell. Wow! Where would I start?

But I did. For the entire hour, I described our thirty-two years of marriage—being parents to our son, problems with family, our professions, and the love we had shared. From those moments of conversation, I discovered deep feelings, which started to well up, and came out through tears and laughter. The happiness we had shared was foremost, and talking about it was a good thing.

Afterward, I remember feeling hope and joy. For the remainder of that day, I found myself giggling at a particular memory. I even had energy to go shopping and out to dinner with my dear friend Gwen. That session was a turning point in my grief journey, perhaps perfectly timed by a very astute counselor. Through this sharing, I was on my way to identifying ME, Maryann Hartzell.

Eddie, I know you believe in the value of counseling. I hope you too have a therapist who is helping you to identify yourself in this new life journey.

Talk to you soon, dear friend.

WEEK THIRTY-THREE

Sleep and Signs

My dear Eddie,

I hope you are well as you continue on your journey of firsts this year. I hope you are sleeping and waking up refreshed with few dreams. I want to write about that today. When you read this letter, you will relate this story to a previous one about signs from our husbands.

I know my sleep was different many nights. I do not remember dreaming a lot, but often upon waking, I needed a few minutes to register in my mind how my life had changed. Coming out of a deep sleep with a jolt, I was back in reality.

I do remember one morning waking from a dream about John. Usually, if I did dream, he was sick. However, this day, tall and dressed in a white shirt and colorful tie, he bent down to kiss me. I saw a slight smile on his face as we said good-bye. When looking back, I cherish that morning. I allowed myself to receive a message that he was not sick anymore. He was healthy again and doing one of his favorite things. He was going to work!

My counselor interpreted the dream in a similar way. She suggested that John was telling me he was safe and not to worry. Feeling a new calmness, I considered his visit a gift—a special sign just for me that gave me hope. Here is to a great week for you, dearest friend.

Love,

Mary

Herschell

My dear Eddie,

As you know, my beloved Herschell died this week. I know he was a dog, but he was many other things too. I know you understand because you have always had dogs. Now in your life, a dog keeps you safe.

The grief I feel today brings back the hours and days after John died. My stomach feels like a tight fist that lets up for a while and then clenches down on me. I feel its grip on my soul as tears flow often, accelerating into sobs. After years without John, I again know that pain will subside one day, but not for a while.

In January 1999, four months after John died, we had to put Crackers, our old dog, to sleep. He had become ill at the kennel, and the kids picked him up. I was in Florida, having accepted an invitation for New Year's Eve at my brother's home. My flights were canceled for two days because of huge snowstorms, and knowing what was going on at home was stressful, to say the least.

When I finally got home, seeing how sick our dog was, I called our veterinarian. He urged me to bring Crackers to the clinic. Kindly, he said, "It is time, Mrs. Hartzell."

Sadly, we all drove together, held him, and cried over him. The struggle was over, with no more pills, no more sickness, and no more sleepless nights. After about an hour, J.T. said, "Let's go to the bar. Enough sadness!" We did! Over a cold

beer, we toasted Crackers, John, and all the great memories we had as a family.

Now, with the loss of my Herschell, the hurt rises up in my throat. I find myself numb, not hungry, and low on energy. Truly, these are physical symptoms of grief. Once again, I feel their pulling force.

The real feeling I have is missing him. I know intellectually that when a person or pet dies after being sick, it is a release from pain and suffering. Yet I know that mourning for as long as it takes is okay. No timelines, just moving slowly through the coming days.

This week I devote this letter in memory of Herschell. How lucky we have been to love, Eddie.

Loving you,

Familiarity

My dearest friend,

I have been thinking about you. In our last conversation, you mentioned that Realtors were coming to look at your home. I am wondering how that went. Selling the house is a big step, and you will know when the time is right!

Thinking back on decisions, I need to acknowledge familiarity. I think that being in places that feel familiar is important. Though this sounds trivial, one of the familiar things in my life was a silver chipmunk that resided happily under our front porch.

During the weeks of John's illness, my morning started with the chipmunk's sitting on the concrete step, chirping loudly. Sometimes his voice was so shrill it woke us up! The familiarity of this continued after John died. I rather regarded this little rodent as a friend.

Then one morning, there was no chirping. When I looked out onto the porch, there was no silver chipmunk. As the day continued, thoughts of him came and went. Early that evening, several of my friends picked me up, and we went out to dinner. We had fun, laughing about the latest epic in one of our lives. It felt good to laugh!

After they dropped me off, I went for a short walk. The moon was full, with long streams of yellow light bouncing off the earth. A few birds were quietly singing, perhaps a lullaby,

as I finished my walk by circling our house.

When I was just about done checking on my gardens and still enjoying the brightness of the moon, I looked down on a white stone. There, lying as if sleeping, was the chipmunk. His eyes were closed, his body, relaxed, and the reality of what I was witnessing sunk into my thoughts.

How he died was not my concern. Perhaps a cat got to him, or perhaps it was just his time. I lingered, looking at his still form. Even though life had left him, he still reflected beauty in the moonlight. His shiny coat appeared shinier, and the memory of his cheerful chirping rang in my ears. He, part of my familiarity, now was in the past.

As you and I know, life changes, and life does go on. However, I believe the gifts of familiarity take the sharp edges away, smoothing them. When you walk through your home, many familiar things are around you. All of this provides a wonderful sense of security.

I believe in you, dear friend. I know you appreciate the familiar, but slowly you are readying yourself for future life. Even though you might move away, you will take familiar objects, including memories, with you. Together they will create a new home filled with love.

Missing you today, dear friend,

The Beginning of Me from We

My dearest Eddie,

The first letter I wrote to you was about Chuck's funeral. Over the months, I have shared many stories and experiences. This story today seems appropriate and a perfect place to insert its meaning. It took place on the day of my John's funeral.

John kept spare change, ticket stubs, and other mementoes from events in the bottom drawer of his dresser. He would jokingly say, "Mary, I have to clean this out before I die." He never did.

After the funeral, the kids dropped me off, and I was alone in the house. For some reason, I remember thinking about that dresser drawer. Climbing the stairs to our bedroom, I decided to clean out its contents. Do not ask me why I felt I should do this, but I did. Sitting down, cushioned by the soft carpeting, I pulled out the drawer and looked in on a lot of . . . stuff.

There were old letters; brochures from last year's boat show; dog-eared pictures of our son in T-ball; John's favorite picture of me, skinny and nineteen years old, wearing a flip coiffeur hairstyle; many non-paired athletic socks; dry cleaning stubs; and a set of luggage tags. These all crowded a space reflecting years of accumulation, years of my husband's life!

Emptying the contents gave me a sense of control—a sense of control I had not felt for a long time. I probably said to myself that this should have been done before, so now it was getting done.

Next, I went down to the kitchen. After opening the refrigerator door and pulling the wastebasket over, I started to select food items that John had always loved. After a few minutes, the shelves looked empty. Now I was rid of foods that I would not need. Neither would John!

In that instant, the reality of the last few days hit me. I remember closing an open window and . . . screaming! I do not know how long this continued, only that the sound came from my toes. Later, spent, I sat down in the middle of the room and surrendered to the moment.

I was alone. Alone without John. He was gone. He was not coming back.

Darkness came, and I ventured back up to our bedroom. I opened the shared closet we had used for twenty years. John's shirts hung, pressed, ready to be worn. Pants folded over wooden hangers accompanied by brightly designed ties hung vertically against the wall.

My clothes were across from his. I proceeded to remove John's things, and took them down the hall to our son's old bedroom closet. After several trips, hours later, our closet still held a hint of my husband's aftershave, but his clothes were no longer visible. In actuality, the closet was . . . mine.

I was exhausted and physically spent, and the day was over. After showering and climbing into our bed, I lay there thinking.

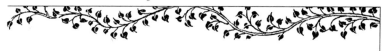

For some reason, I had started to make changes. These changes were for me. The beginning of my new journey alone had begun.

Eddie, I haven't thought about that day for a long time. Thank you for listening.

Loving you, dear friend.

WEEK THIRTY-SEVEN

Father's Day

My dearest Eddie,

Our first Father's Day without John presented with beautiful sunshine and singing birds . . . yes, many cardinals! Plans for the day included the kids' coming over for church, followed by brunch. We did just that and had a nice time. "Nice" is a good, safe word describing our activities.

We drove to the cemetery, bringing a colorful bouquet of daisies. Putting them on the grave, there was little conversation as the three of us stood, looking at the stone. J.T. polished away a film of dirt as I placed the flowers in a vase, and Kelly picked up twigs and clipped grass. We all were busy, lost in our own thoughts as we cried softly.

As if I knew this would happen, I had prepared something special. After returning to the car, I put in a CD by John Denver. He sang about family and babies, but mostly about love. Sitting in our separate places in the front seats and backseat, we wept while listening to the poignant lyrics. It was good time spent together quietly, sharing memories.

When we got back home, the kids stayed a little while, then left. I got out my special box of family pictures, old cards, and J.T.'s baby book. I spent the rest of the afternoon sitting in the warm sunshine, reliving the many Father's Days we had experienced as a family. I thanked God for the gift of sharing parenthood with my husband. I do believe that

having a child together is the greatest experience possible in a marriage.

As the sun set, I felt happy with the way we had lived the day. Now, many years later, J.T., Kelly, and I remember how we celebrated it together.

So here is to another first this year, Eddie.

Love,

Mary

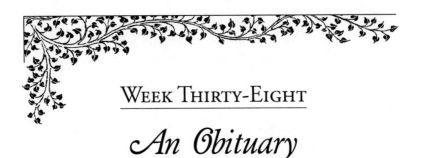

Week Thirty-Eight

An Obituary

My dear Eddie,

I am writing today about creating an obituary. The one I am using is for my beloved Herschell. Its focus is telling the reader about him and who loved him. I wish more obituaries were this personal. Here it is:

At ten o'clock in the morning on Monday, June 4, 2012, my devoted friend passed away. Surrounded by his family, he left this world to cross over the bridge into heaven. He was ninety-one years old, and had shiny gray hair, deep brown eyes, and a voice that could be heard for several blocks. He loved to play his saxophone and could toss the football at least four feet in the air. His favorite treat was pepperoni sticks, and he preferred hard food to soft, even in old age.

After his last dental cleaning, he had six teeth, so when he smiled, his two large upper front teeth slid over his bottom lip. His tongue frequently snuck out of his mouth when he was sleeping, causing a soft snore that filled a room. Always the first to go to bed, he was also the first to wake up in the morning. He did not walk; he galloped, stopping at high structures, leaving a mark for others who would follow in his steps.

My friend knew me better than anyone else. We were friends all of his life, and he helped me through both happy and sad times. He was there to share changes in my life, even if he was just sitting by me.

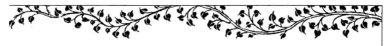

Our time together started in November, thirteen years ago. His first Thanksgiving was spent in Florida, and we flew down together in an airplane. He loved the snacks onboard, especially the bottled water and pretzel sticks. Many trips to Florida followed, but because of his height, eventually, he had to fly in the lower compartment of the plane. Once we became separated when the airline booked him on a different flight. I will always remember our reunion in Daytona Beach. We were thrilled to see each other again.

My friend's name was Herschell. That name means dependable, strong, and trustworthy. He lived up to that name. When he was two years old, his sister had her first family. I adopted Henrietta, who was his niece. She adored him, only giving him a hard time if he got near her ice cream.

We saw each other every day. Thus, we shared many adventures. I would like to retell a few of them so that you really know Herschell Hartzell-Curran. After you read these stories, I think you will agree that he was special.

We met through a good friend who knew Herschell's cousin. You could tell that they were related because of their good nature, great energy, and love of escapades. He was very seldom sad, and the legacy of his family followed him through his whole life. He and Henrietta were quite a team, like Lady and the Tramp. She will miss his presence in her life.

Herschell loved to take his naps in the afternoon, securely perched on the living room sofa. Even when the household was busy, it was easy to find him because he was always there. He preferred riding in golf carts instead of cars. When we had our condominium on the ocean, he loved to go up and down in the elevator, and rode on the portable grocery cart as often as

he could. Once he ran down the lawn and out onto the beach, where he stopped in amazement at all the blue water. That same weekend, he rushed to the sliding patio door, alerting us to two lost crabs knocking on the window. When we all looked at their lifted claws as they danced back and forth, getting close to them was not an option.

Herschell was very protective of us all. Being a true friend, he often went first into new situations. If he saw potential visitors coming up the front sidewalk, he always let us know someone was at the door. When the guests came into the living room, he was gracious, running to get a toy to share if they cared to play. If not, he rested near all the conversation, content just to be near the family.

When we had been gone, he was the first to get up and welcome us home, acting as if we were the most important people in the world. Feeling like royalty, we were treated to his unconditional love time and again. I would frequently walk over a warm spot in my bare feet, knowing he had been waiting until our return. Now that is a devoted, patient friend!

He was healthy most of his life, and the diagnosis of a heart valve problem did not seem to faze him. He took his medicine, often coupled with liver sausage, never sharing any of that treat with Henrietta. His first medical event, years ago, occurred on a trip to Florida when he ate something native and nasty. My friend Mary Jane, a retired nurse, saved the day with an old remedy, hydrogen peroxide. Being Herschell, he still loved her, but for a while from a distance!

Early this summer, he became weak, had little appetite, and had trouble sleeping. Frequent visits to the doctor some-times became a daily ritual. Each time, we would return

home with new medicine, instructions, and assurance that he still had "quality of life."

Then the day came when he no longer had that quality, and our doctor told us lovingly that it was his "time."

We rode together for that last appointment. Jack drove, while Henrietta, Herschell, and I clung jointly in the backseat. My tears flowed as my heart started to break. I had a bottle of water nestled in my purse, and I filled a capful, trying to have Herschell drink the warm liquid. However, he could not. Instead, when drops spilled on my leg, he licked them lovingly. Now, in telling the story, I think he was saying good-bye, knowing his time with us was ending. He was far braver than we were, but remember, he was Herschell.

An hour later, the three of us returned home. Herschell had died peacefully in our arms. Our doctor had assured us that we could come retrieve his ashes on Wednesday afternoon. We did, receiving them in a beautiful cedar box embossed with his name.

In closing, I hope you have gotten a glimpse into life with Herschell Hartzell-Curran. Though he is no longer here physically, I know he is spiritually. Looking around our house, I feel his presence, knowing how blessed we were to have him in our lives. For now, I can say, "Good-bye, my beloved Herschell." I know in my heart that we will meet again as we cross the rainbow bridge together because there is a heaven . . . for dogs. Loving you, Eddie,

The Fourth of July

My dear Eddie,

By the time you read this letter, July 4 will have passed. To be honest, I do not remember a lot about the first one without John, but I do have memories of the last one with him.

The Fourth of July was one of John's favorite holidays. When we were dating, one of our highlights was lighting sparklers and holding them until they almost burned our fingers. Then, through the years, we participated in many parades and gave festive parties. He and my brother, Russ, used to have a phenomenal annual display on the lake, delighting all of us. But this last Fourth was different. He wasn't feeling well, so we stayed home. I remember making a simple supper for us both. No more barbecue on our grill; no more decorating with colorful flags along our sidewalk. Instead, we spent the day reminiscing about all the Fourths we had celebrated. We went to bed early.

After awakening around ten o'clock, with John sleeping peacefully, I left our bed. I walked into the guest room and sat by a window. The bedroom blinds were drawn, so all I heard was the explosion of fireworks. Seeming to be all around, the noise came from many directions. I chose not to open the blinds and look out. I was content to hear, not see, the displays.

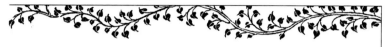

Looking back, I think the sudden change from our normal celebrations left me depressed. For some unknown reason, I remembered a red, white, and blue Jello mold I had made for a party years ago. Then I started crying softly, letting the tears fall on my robe. I felt the sadness, along with the reality of life ahead. After a while, I walked back to bed, quickly falling asleep. The sound of John's steady breathing almost sang to me like a lullaby.

I think this experience made me more appreciative of the time we had left. The next weekend, our son was married, and the special happiness we felt was inexplicable. The church was packed with people we loved and who loved us. The minister whispered to me, "This many people never come to a wedding. They usually show up at the reception." What joy! We were thrilled to celebrate together.

Maybe, dearest friend, we must have the quiet, sad time before the happy time. When my niece married on the Fourth of July in 2010, I again felt John's presence. She and her new husband had an exploding backdrop behind them, filling the night with bright starbursts of color.

Admiring the colliding explosions of fireworks streaming across the sky, I remembered the other Fourth of July celebrations. Perhaps John was helping with all of this happiness and sharing it from heaven! I wouldn't be surprised!

Loving you,

Renewal of My Grief

Dear Eddie,

As you know, Herschell died on June 4. Because this has been incredibly hard, my counselor suggested I write about my feelings. She thought this might be the perfect time to insert these thoughts amongst the letters. Therefore, I am doing this with a lump in my throat.

We all know cognitively that time heals everything. Why? is an interesting question. Is it because other things take over, and life goes on? I know intellectually that time does go on and people do go on, but in the depths of grief, it is hard to rationalize why.

Herschell was invested in so much of my past, present, and future. I guess I never thought he could die—"could" is a good word. Then, I did not think John would die or could die either. I think when Herschell died, so much from John's death reappeared, hence this tremendous grief. I know I will get through this, but I do not know when, or for how long I will feel deep sadness.

I think grief fools us. If we are lucky, we have a break between each individual instance of grief. I did for four months after John's death, and then our old dog, Crackers, died. I had little grief until my father-in-law passed away, a year after John. When I got my Herschell, somehow he made grief almost impossible because of the joy he brought to my life. Now he is gone, and I am left to accept reality.

Many e-mails, cards, and letters have been sent. Each one is special because it shares the love and loss of Herschell. I made a binder and filled it with these pieces of correspondence. The beauty of caring people, especially pet lovers, was the thread of love woven into their words.

Last Sunday, I was in the lowest point of my grief. All the feelings of loss bombarded my very being. I did not get dressed, shower, or go out all day. It was almost as if I needed to just feel. It was very painful, but my counselor cautioned me not to backpedal or think I had failed in healing from all the years back. She made an interesting statement, questioning if we actually ever finish grieving.

Instead, we go on bruised, but when healed, allow ourselves to feel again. Maybe, we even take a chance to love once more. Something to ponder!

Today is Friday. I feel better and was able to exercise and do errands. I know there is still a long way to go, but for the moment—and I mean moment—I feel peace. One thing I need to remember is not to look too far ahead, but just go day by day. Another is not to go too far back until I am stronger. My goal is feeling the loss but also celebrating the present, enjoying Henrietta and Jack.

I am thankful for so many things. God blessed me with a dog named Herschell. He allowed me to love and be loved. Long ago, I read the anonymous statement, "One day all love stories will come to an end." However, my John and Herschell love stories will never end; they will live on in my memory and also in my heart forever.

Dearest friend, thank you for listening.

Love,

Mary

Water, Water Everywhere

My dear Eddie,

One day about a month before John died, we had returned from the doctor. After driving through a huge rainstorm with our street flooded and bolts of lightning bursting like firecrackers, we arrived home.

I had John settled into his favorite chair and our old dog nestled at his feet, and I suddenly had this sixth sense. I felt the need to journey down into our basement. After opening the door, I proceeded down the steps. Suddenly, my foot touched dampness that became inches of water. As I continued, dread was setting in because I realized our basement was flooded!

A sliver of light up at the top of the stairs flickered on and off, turning into darkness. The power was out! I knew that I had to fix this problem. Swishing through the water, I found the fuse box. I opened the cold metal door and started frantically moving the switches back and forth. Nothing happened! Frustrated, I made my way back up the swollen steps, climbed to the top, and opened the door as the kitchen filled with light!

Proud of myself, I then roused John from his sleep. His eyes lit up as I told the story wearing a smug smile on my face. "You did what to the fuse box?" he exclaimed.

"Mary, you could have been electrocuted!" Then we both started to cry.

Perhaps in that moment, all of our emotions asserted the reality of our situation. I knew that my actions could have caused a catastrophe, and so did John. Now, looking back, I know God was in the basement standing next to me. He was protecting us both, and I will always be thankful for His care.

Eddie, this is yet another "lightning day" story. That experience taught me to be more careful, even cautious. I must have learned a lesson because I am retelling this story years later. In fact, I had a similar experience the first spring after John died, but that is another story!

Keep dry, my friend. Maybe it is good that we have no basements in Florida.

Love you,

Mary

My Boat Story

My dearest friend,

It is a cool, misty, rainy day, perhaps a good one for my boat story. This kind of weather reminds me of our boating days. I am sure you agree since a lot of your boating was on Lake Michigan. One minute all is perfect, like the Sea of Galilee with Jesus in the boat, and then a storm out of nowhere rocks you around.

About two months after John died, I put the boat on the market. It took a year to sell. Truly, boating was a we thing, and our we was no more.

The last weekend we went to the boat, John was weak. However, beloved boat club friends helped get him settled on the living room sofa. My best sense told me to ask him where everything was located—batteries, instructions, tools, etc. Man stuff. Well, after he looked at me, shrugging his shoulders, my questions were answered. Then John rested. When we left that afternoon, I felt relief and a sense of accomplishment. This helped overshadow the sorrow of reality that filled my heart. We would never return to the boat together.

About a month after the funeral, my friend Joanne came to visit, and we drove to the boat. I parked the car in front of the slip and walked ahead of her down the dock. Starting up the steps to enter the boat, I froze. A grief coming from my toes spilled over me. I felt a cold chill as we unsnapped the aft cover. Joanne literally held me up as I collapsed in her arms.

It was the next best thing to having John there. In fact, thinking back, he was there—through her.

We stayed only long enough to pack clothes and personal items in a few boxes. We walked around, sharing the memories of all the boating we had done on vacations together. We laughed a little. Then I stopped talking.

Suddenly, I had nothing to say. Joanne accepted this in me. She drove home, made my dinner, and put me to bed that night. Looking back, I feel this was a pivotal time in my grief. I was forced to accept that our boating days were gone, and so was my beloved John.

This loss of words lasted three days. When Joanne left, I was sitting in our family room rocking chair, warmed by sun coming into the windows. She cried hard, saying, "I wish there was something I could do." Eddie, you and I know that there was not anything, except to feel the pain. I will always love her for her care.

Days passed. I remember little, except the importance of being quiet in our home, just breathing. Of course, I did start to talk again, to venture out, and to live, but I needed to shut down for a while. I am thankful for those days, for that time alone. Those hours and days were part of my healing, and only God and I could do it together.

Within a year's time, the boat did sell. I was able to put this chapter of my life away in a safe place, along with a generous check. We were so blessed to both have captains in our lives, sharing their love of boating with us. I picture both Chuck and John in safe harbor in heaven. That is a wonderful thought! I like that.

Until next week, dear friend,

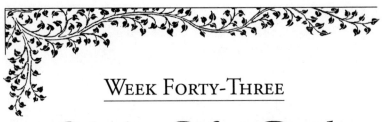

Grieving Before Death

My dear friend,

I think the subject of today's letter is appropriate at this time in your first year. I want to write about grieving before your spouse dies. It happened to me, and I am sure, to you. In fact, I think this is common among caregivers.

You and I were fortunate that our husbands were not "sick" for a long time. Granted, our lives changed with different treatments, side effects, and medication, but our husbands' time of incapacity was short. I remember when a doctor said John was not "sick" yet. Several months later, he was.

Perhaps a certain reality sets in with the caregiver. One time, John said he thought it was easier to be the patient than the one caring for an ill person. When I asked him to describe why, he said because the caretaker does lots of worrying, and the patient is just trying to get better. There is truth in those words.

Each year we hosted a Christmas party for the business, and we did our last Christmas. I remember talking with our partners' wives, one being a nurse. She made a comment, "How are you doing? Trying to keep your chins up?"

At that moment, I did not know how to respond. I am sure I denied this, saying something like, "We are doing fine."

Days later, after a doctor's appointment, John and I went shopping. I remember walking through Marshall Field's,

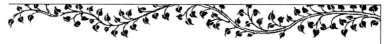

commenting on this and that. Each time I did, John had the clerk ring up the items I liked. When I noted the expensive prices, John laughed, "It is only money, Mary."

During our marriage, I started a beautiful collection of Christmas dinnerware made by Lenox. On another day when we were shopping, John ordered the sugar bowl and matching creamer, knowing these pieces would complete my set. The clerk raised an eyebrow, saying, "Sir, this sugar bowl is seventy-five dollars."

John said, "Where do I sign?" Giggling happily, we left the department embracing our purchases.

Living with cancer teaches you to enjoy the highs and endure the lows, living day to day. I emphasize live. The last week of John's life, I remember cherishing each hour. Simple activities, such as eating dinner and sleeping in our bed together each night, held vast importance. I think about one of our last mornings; when opening my eyes, I saw tears rolling down John's cheek. With our arms around each other, holding each other close, we admired the rising sun seen through our bedroom window. I think by now, John had accepted his diagnosis, already missing his family as well as the beauty of our earth. But I truly believe John knew he was going to heaven. Days later, in those last few seconds of his life, we all saw the radiant smile on his face. He saw something in the distance, and I believe it was our Father.

God must feel sad looking down at His children as they struggle. I think even in His infinite wisdom, He sheds tears.

When He brings us together to start a love story, He knows one day it must end. One partner will leave a

marriage and leave the other alone. But going on with memories and the love of our God makes living possible!

Personally, I look at grieving before death as a gift, one that people do not have when death is sudden. Illness can be this gift in its own way, allowing us to share, say good-byes, and appreciate the little things in life. As hard as all of this is, the time before death helps us see each other in a different way.

Perhaps God's love shines more brightly during this pre-grief period. Perhaps reaching out for His hand in our darkest hours is a reality, one to be taken advantage of if possible. I think He holds us while we learn to accept that our lives will change very soon.

Eddie, this is my story for week forty-three. I know you will relate to its message.

Loving you,

Mary

Anger With Professionals

Dearest Eddie,

As you know, some of my letters have described how I dealt with anger. There was anger during the clothes distribution, even anger cleaning out the refrigerator after John's funeral. Today, I want to write about my anger at the end of John's treatments.

After John's fourth recurrence of his cancer, our doctor recommended he be part of a research program. The hospital offering a trial drug was located in downtown Chicago. Before the last administration of the trial drug, John had a brain scan. By then, we were used to these tests, accepting them as part of the program. However, this was the first brain scan he had had for a year. Naturally, we were apprehensive.

The afternoon we visited the doctor, he had results from all the tests except that scan. During our conversation, the news that cancer had invaded John's left lung became our next hurdle. With compassion, the doctor left us in the examining room to absorb this information. He returned within a few minutes to suggest another treatment. Later, we left the hospital, crestfallen and scared.

During the next week, we waited for the doctor's call sharing the brain scan results. However, no call ever came.

Two weeks later, in the early morning hours, John awoke suffering his first brain seizure. Thus began the final road of

our journey. At our local hospital, after a terrifying ride in the ambulance, it was confirmed by X-ray that the cancer was in his brain.

As our world collapsed around us, many questions arose in my mind, one being, "Where was the brain scan that was taken weeks ago?" Our local doctor made calls to the research facility. He was told that yes, the X-ray had been found and placed in the wrong doctor's mailbox. The hospital apologized!

Months went by; more questions arose in my mind as I adjusted to life without my husband. Rather than calming me, the passing time fueled my anger. Intellectually, I knew there would be no peace until I contacted the research doctor myself. The final assault was in the form of a collection letter from the hospital for seventy-five dollars. After I opened the statement, my fury took over, literally making me scream! How dare they!

"Hello," said a meek voice. "I am so glad you called me, Mrs. Hartzell." As angry as I felt, as tired as I was, I was thankful to hear our doctor's voice. The conversation began, and he allowed, yes, allowed, me to unload, to vent, and to cry. He assured me that research requirements had changed and that John's participation already had helped others. Most important to me was his promise to never lose an X-ray again—to always pursue lost test results so that what happened to us would never happen to another family.

After talking for several more minutes, we said good-bye. As I hung up the receiver, I felt peace finally settling over me. I believe God gave me the strength and courage to make

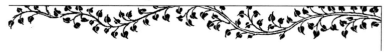

that call. Finally, I had the closure needed to go on with my questions answered.

Eddie, whether anger plays a big or small part in your grief journey is up to you. I do believe being honest with yourself and accepting its presence helps in the change from WE to ME.

Love you, dearest friend.

Mary

WEEK FORTY-FIVE

The Cardinals

My dearest friend,

I am writing this on a stormy Friday afternoon, understanding that the forecast calls for rain all weekend. Bummer! It's a great day to write a letter to my friend.

I hope all is well as you make decisions on your own. Bearing this in mind, my letter today is yet another sign story. I think you might find it familiar since our friendship over the years shared this theme.

My mom died when I was thirty-two years old. In fact, it was the same year you and I met. Now, thirty-five years later, a promise she made to us is still coming true.

Mother loved birds. She especially loved cardinals and always enjoyed their gaiety, beauty, and chirping voices. Once she told us that if she came back to earth after death, she would be a cardinal!

I think she kept her promise. Many events in my life, both happy and sad, have included a visit from the cardinal. Impossible to count, the appearances of the red bird are numerous, but each is separately poignant. The most recent experience was on the Monday morning our beloved Herschell died.

Standing at the kitchen window, I was alerted to the familiar voice of the cardinal. Within seconds, two females and a male perched on our white front porch fence. Of course, my tears

really flowed, but with a sense of security. Could it be my mother once again nurturing me through the birds?

When I have shared cardinal stories with my sister and brother, they have related similar sightings from their lives. What a gift to the three of us from a loving parent.

That is my story this week—another sign of love from a loved one. When I think back on the first year without John, I saw cardinals at least once a week. They were especially prevalent when I was making an important decision. I pictured my mom and John looking down, hands on their hips and releasing a cardinal to remind me of their presence.

Hope you are well, dear friend.

Love,

Mary

WEEK FORTY-SIX

Experiencing the Pain

My dearest Eddie,

When I think of an analogy about grief, I need to emphasize the importance of going through the pain . . . not around it. My personal description is this:

"Grief is like diving into the deep end of a pool, swimming underwater, arriving at the shallow end, and being able to walk out into the sunlight." This word picture hopefully illustrates my experiences with grief.

The first Christmas after John died, I read an ad in our local paper. The Jewel Supermarket was looking for a salesperson to run its floral department. Interviewing for the job, I was ready to accept the position. Later, I called my attorney and asked his opinion. His concern was about the many days when I might be unstable and making errors in judgment. Hanging up the phone, I said to myself, "Not me."

However, the next morning, I awoke to a dark, rainy day, which provoked my sadness. The tears flowed freely, helping me to make the right decision. Late that afternoon, I called the Human Resources Department, saying no to the job offer.

There are so many ups and downs in grieving. As you know, a song, a memory, a sunset can make you cry. There were days when I wore no eye makeup. I didn't even carry tissues. Instead, I let the tears fall down my face, giving myself permission to mourn.

At first, there was a sharp pain in my heart. Losing John was different from the loss of my parents. This new pain caused me to be hopeless. When my mom and dad died, it was hard, but I always had John there with me. Now John was gone. I knew he was no longer suffering, but I was still here, hurting.

I believe that feelings must be felt, even though the pain can rip you apart. Now, years later, I promise people new in their grief that they will heal. Having a loving support system will enable you to be happy again. You and I are blessed with such an environment, Eddie.

Take care, dearest friend.

Mary

Week Forty-Seven

I Did It My Way

Dearest friend,

"I Did It My Way" rings in my ears as I write this. I think this song's lyrics are poignant, with the singer giving, and the audience receiving a message. Frank Sinatra must have known the music could affect many lives.

Early in John's treatment, we were told about aggressive chemotherapy available in a hospital setting. I was ready to pump all the medicine on the market into his body, hoping to rid him of this terrible disease. However, he was not. Instead, John decided to use a more docile, less invasive therapy, so we did.

As the years progressed, the recurrences happened, and I fought being angry, even resentful. I learned to honor the decisions, praying he was satisfied with the choices. We continued to fight each rising of the cancer and, for the most part, were a team in quest for an end to the disease. However, that was not meant to be.

After John died and I heard this song, I had many feelings. I respect individual thoughts and choices. However, when you are involved in a couple relationship, shouldn't you think about that instead of your own desires? I dwelled on that subject for a long time.

Yet now, when I think back, I know John needed to live the way he wanted until he could not anymore. We always

made plans, never giving up the possibility that there was not a long future ahead of us. Our vacations, the purchase of a new boat, and awaiting our son's wedding gave focus and meaning to the time ahead.

Along with the drugs, the hopes and dreams we lived kept him going. I am glad that he did what he did, and we did what we did. Years later, it all makes sense.

Love is complicated. Love is complex. Love is going the extra distance in order to accept the choices your husband is making and can live with. Perhaps the word "live" is the main word. In a way, that is the real gift of relationship that many people will never experience. My friend, I think both of us had strong husbands who did it their way.

In closing, I want to say that even though we are not with them anymore, they left knowing we were supporting their decisions. I think we were blessed with them, and they, with us.

Here is to love, dear friend.

How Will I Live Without You?

My dearest friend,

I remember walking with John on a cold Sunday afternoon in early January. When I look back, it was the year before he got sick. Twilight was setting in as the temperature started to drop. We were not cold because our walk had invigorated even our toes. Enjoying the fresh air as our old dog romped like a puppy in the white paradise, we started toward home.

As we approached the end of the road, lying there in a ditch was the body of a Canadian goose. Its feathers moved gently in the soft wind; there was nothing around it except fresh snow. Off in the distance, I saw a solitary goose stand gazing in our direction. We both stopped.

"I understand that geese mate for life," I muttered in the deep stillness.

John wagged his head, standing next to me. "Yes, I have heard that too," he answered. We both were sad, reaching for each other's gloved hand.

In the next instant, I said, "We are so lucky. You have not had a recurrence this year. Isn't it great that we do not have to worry about cancer anymore?"

John was quiet. "Oh, Mary, I never stop thinking about cancer," he said quietly. I was surprised.

This story remains in my memory of special moments. I think back on that afternoon, when we were sharing our love story and comparing it to the parted geese. Even though they were not humans, they had an arrangement for life that now was interrupted. Little did I know that in less than one year, our lives would radically change too!

I think of all the songs written expressing the question, "How will I live without you?" Often movie themes build their plots around this dilemma. I guess the bottom line is people are curious. Think about all the couples who celebrate fifty, sixty, and even seventy years of marriage together. A couple in our church recently announced their seventieth anniversary. Unbelievable, but true!

While John was sick, I did not really allow myself to think about this question. We were busy living. Dying was not part of our daily thoughts. Perhaps I was more unrealistic than I should have been. I guess when you second-guess yourself, lots of "could'ves" and "should'ves" cross your mind.

Yes, Eddie, as you and I know, life does go on. The sun always comes up in the morning and goes down at night. The moon rises and disappears, the birds sing, people go to work, and babies are born. Life does go on, even if you think yours has stopped. Though your husband's heart no longer beats, yours does. Remember the old song "The Beat Goes On"? It will!

I believe the first year alone is literally a series of firsts accomplished through love, faith, and patience. At the end, going into the second year, life will be more realistic. You have proved that life is going on, sweetened by wonderful memories of your marriage. Any regrets will be less bitter

as the days go by. My regret was that there was not enough time—we would never be married fifty years!

Therefore, my dearest friend, perhaps even though geese and people can mate for life, there are interruptions to this natural flow. It is up to the living to keep on living. In my first year, I lived for both John and me. Now, I live for myself, knowing one day in heaven, we will be together again. I am comforted by this promise of a God who loves us.

Always love,

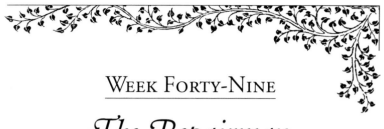

WEEK FORTY-NINE

The Repairman

My dearest friend,

I know you are chuckling as you look at this title. This next story will make you smile, but I know you will identify with its message too.

Remember the flooded basement story? Six months after John died, after a terrible storm, I heard water rushing somewhere. Of course, I suspected the basement! Down the steps I ventured, and I found a window leaking in John's workshop. I put rags around the leak and went back upstairs . . . to open the Yellow Pages.

"24 Hour Emergency Service" in large type stared up at me. I called. A voice, human, not a computer, answered on the third ring. "Yes," a person would be able to come in a few hours. I kept changing the wet, saturated rags, waiting anxiously to hear the doorbell. When the bell rang, I ran up the stairs.

An older man stood on the front porch. I invited him in, and we proceeded down the basement steps. Feeling awkward, I thought I was taking a perfect stranger into the lowest level of the house. I quickly reminded myself that there was no time for such thoughts!

The man assured me of his expertise. As he walked around the basement, checking corners, remaining windows, and the concrete walls, he presented me with his opinion. "I think the

best remedy is to jackhammer the four corners of the house foundation. We will re-level the structure, and I assure you, there will be no more water problems." I thought I heard the house groan!

Looking back at that morning, I am sure my face fell five feet. The next comment from him was on price. "I am quoting you three thousand dollars for this job, but it could be more!" He smirked after these words. Continuing, he said, "If you give me a check today, I will knock off 10 percent."

Now time for me to smirk! "Sir, with all due respect, I need to ask my son for his opinion, and I will get back to you." Chagrined, he left, and my next call was to my neighbor. He gave me the name of a repairman in the area, one his family had used. So I called. The next day, that recommended repairman came, re-caulked the window, and charged me three hundred dollars. I know the house was smiling. I was!

My son said later that he was proud of me and thankful for my common sense. We also were happy to have a dry basement!

Eddie, we can be "victims" of repair people. Yet we need to have good, reliable ones who make staying in our homes possible. I know you have common sense. In fact, I can hear you laughing as I share this story. By now, you must have stories too! The great thing about Florida is that we have no basements!

Love you, dear friend.

WEEK FIFTY

Moving On

My dearest friend,

As we approach the end of your first year without Chuck, I want to share another story in my transition from WE to ME.

Our attorney, now my attorney, gave me an excellent piece of advice several months after John died. Staying in the home we had shared for at least the first year was his recommendation. At first I was offended that he would even think that I would want to move. In actuality, though, I kept our family home for two years before selling.

During those years, I continued to find comfort in all the memories made in the house. I did, however, make changes. I had wallpaper and new windows installed, and I put comfortable new furniture in our family room. These changes not only upgraded this twenty-three-year-old structure, but also helped in making our home mine.

Two years allowed me to begin changes for myself, yet enjoy the familiarity the house represented. Remember the story about our home being like a friend wrapping her arms around you? Well, that was true! When I decided to sell, the decision was not made in haste. I believe you know when the time comes because it must be your choice.

Moving was a huge decision involving emptying closets, and cleaning out the basement and the garage. The kids helped me decide about family items that were kept, donated, or discarded. Working together really made all of

this easier, bonding us closer as a family.

Even Herschell helped! Finding a long-dead mouse in a basement corner, he galloped around the house, displaying his prize. Much needed laughter embraced us all as the three of us chased this playful puppy. I really think John might have put Herschell up to this prank. It was a fun moment!

A great investment was the rental of a large trash receptacle from a local refuse company. It was delivered and placed on our driveway. Not only was this bin convenient for throwing things away; it provided a catharsis of release as we "pitched" unwanted items into the large cavern. We all shed lots of tears parting with things that help memories, but the choices also freed us to share what they had meant to us. Two weekends of this work found the house well organized and ready for the next step.

A young couple from Wisconsin bought the house. I actually was given the information about the sale as I sat in church two Sundays later. Kind of a perfect place for such news! As you know, sentimentality plays a big role when your home is on the market, yet the relief of the sale was a wonderful answer to prayer. The family had three children and eventually moved out of Illinois. However, over the years, as we communicated through Christmas cards, they shared their love for our home. Nice story!

Eddie, my dearest friend, you too probably will sell your house and move. I am glad you were able to spend this first year in the home you and Chuck shared. Wherever you live in the future, you will make your house a new home. I am proud of you!

Love,

Mary

What I Learned in My First Year

My dear friend,

I am looking at the title of this piece. We are almost done with your first year, Eddie. It's hard to believe, isn't it? Yet I know there have been days, hours, weeks, even moments that have dragged on and been painful for you. Unfortunately, that is part of this journey. In those dark moments, I hope you knew that all of us who love you held out our arms in comfort. I hope you felt that warmth against your body.

Again, what did I learn? First, I learned that I was one of the lucky ones. My husband and I loved each other until the end. In today's marriages, that is not always the case. In fact, happy marriages are in the minus column these days. Therefore, I was blessed.

I always knew that I was strong—strong-willed, strong-minded, and determined when I sought a goal. Never caught up in the need to always win, I loved the work and energy expended to pursue a dream. On my own, the first year was difficult, but I had life tools to survive. I know you do too.

I learned to be comfortable alone in the car, in the house, and even in a restaurant. Probably the hardest part of being alone was not sharing my life through conversation. However, my Herschell became my partner, always patient with me as

I talked to him. The way he nodded his head, I was sure he understood. John and I had always talked about everything. I think we were best friends filled with trust and admiration for each other. Again, we were blessed.

I learned to really listen to my kids. Their grief, though different from mine, was the same in many ways. We all depended on each other, with good communication on a regular basis. I think we learned to cry together and share stories, and we made regular dates to meet for dinner. This proved to be very helpful in monitoring each other's feelings, even after the first year.

I learned how deep my faith was through prayer, activities with church friends, and worshiping with my son and his family. That church hour allows us to rest in God's strong arms with our church family. I know you too have kept this tradition. We were blessed to have spiritual, loving husbands who still sit silently next to us on a Sunday morning.

I really learned about my close friends. There were several who were only a phone call away and would come by just to say hello. I loved their visits because of their love and willingness to share those lonely hours with me. Their support held me up on many a rainy, dark day in my soul, while the sun shone brightly outdoors.

I learned how to get from place to place. All my life, directions were difficult, so being alone gave me no choice but to be aware of my surroundings. I also made it a prerequisite to take my car in case I had to leave early. Often I made a trial run to a new place, especially if I had to drive after dark. Taking my own car helped give me freedom to abandon situations that were uncomfortable.

I learned the value of exercise. I started with a trainer that year, continuing to this day with walking and lifting weights. I know this made me feel better about myself physically, even though mentally I was a mess some days.

I learned to accept many bad days as being okay. My physical health was unbelievably good those months, but my emotions ran rampant, with no stability at times. I gave myself permission to "suffer" on those days. As the months tumbled by, there were fewer and fewer bad days.

I learned to depend on people helping me. As I said before, I kept all the "helping" professionals in my life that John and I had used. That too gave security blending with familiarity from years past. The ones I use today adapted and grew as I did over time. That's not easy for everyone. As you and I know, change is difficult, even for professionals who had to learn to deal with a strong woman who was not always rational.

My dearest friend, I just reread this letter. Wow, I did learn a lot that first year. I know you have too. I hope the feelings of love, blessings, and life wove a pattern through this letter's message. Remember, we can live the rest of our lives knowing we were the lucky ones!

I love you, Eddie.

The One-Year Anniversary

My dearest Eddie,

When you look at the calendar, I'm sure it is hard to believe one year has passed. Thinking back, I remember days that dragged on and on, followed by those that slipped by unnoticed. The reality is you soon will start your second year without Chuck. You have experienced all the firsts, and I am proud of you, my friend.

I have always savored firsts—the first bite of delicious food, the first look at your grandchild. This last year of firsts is right up there in importance, but in a different way. Now complete, the firsts have become part of the rest of your life.

Remember the cliché, "Today is the first day of the rest of your life"? I am thinking about those words and the truth in the meaning. Let me share with you how the one-year anniversary affected me and my family.

Reviewing how I spent that day brings back so many memories. I planned a party, inviting all the people who had loved, helped, and coaxed me through those 365 days. I am sure you and Chuck were there. A large tent was set up in the backyard, delicious food was served, and various drinks were available. A CD player provided quiet music, and a soft breeze whispered through the evening air.

On our kitchen counter, I had placed our favorite picture of John, lit by a single votive candle. As people entered the front door, they passed, acknowledging his photo, often smiling in reflection of his happy face looking back at them. I know he would have loved the party. After all, John was really the guest of honor, but even now, we all missed his laugh, jokes, and touch.

I frequently looked around, remembering the kindness over the years, but especially this past year. Many meals, cups of coffee, phone calls, and boxes of tissues were shared with these beloved people. As I glided from one person to the next, I tried not to look behind me. At times, I was sure John followed me throughout the evening.

All these people from many parts of our life together were here. Our beloved pastor and his wife lent reverence and, before the blessing, helped witness three cardinals flying through the eaves of the tent. As we bowed our heads, who could have asked for a more poignant beginning to a special night?

As the hours went by and I mingled, sharing stories, I felt a new peace. When the evening ended, the yard brightened by a full moon, crickets chirping to the beat of the music, my kids and I embraced. We had made it through the first year with this lovely party our reward. God had taken care of everything. We were stronger in our unity as the future stood in front of us.

Now we would go into the second year empowered by God's love and also prompted by memories. What better tribute to our beloved husband, father, friend, and neighbor? Each year on the anniversary of John's death, I remember fondly that lovely evening as we celebrated his life.

Last week you shared your plans for Chuck's one-year anniversary. They sound wonderful, and you will be with your family in a favorite place. Great idea, Eddie!

I am proud of you and send my love.

Thanks, Eddie, for listening to all fifty-two stories.

God's blessings will continue to flow in you for the rest of your life.

Love,

CPSIA information can be obtained at www.ICGtesting.com
Printed in the USA
LVOW100704280513

335585LV00001B/1/P